Reading eggs

READING
skills for First Grade

by Sara Leman

Blake
eLEARNING

Welcome to the Reading Eggs Workbook for First Grade!

I know how much you care about giving your child a great start in reading, because I had the EXACT same feeling, too.

I remember life before **Reading Eggs**. Like you, I was determined to give my four kids the BEST start in life, and that meant helping them learn to read.

The problem was, reading is complicated. There are so many skills they need to learn. From phonemic awareness, phonics, sight words, and vocabulary to comprehension and fluency; it's hard to know where to start. And most children need lots of time and a whole lot of repetition to get all these skills in place. If you're busy, this can get very challenging very quickly.

We knew there had to be an easier way. So I used my 25 years of experience in educational publishing, along with the most SOLID scientific research on reading instruction and child motivation, to create the online **Reading Eggs** program.

This reading program completely transformed the way millions of children around the world learned to read. 10 MILLION children to be exact (and counting)!

I witnessed the magic of **Reading Eggs** with my own children. Laughter replaced the tantrums, excitement replaced the tears, and the best part was they were ACTUALLY learning to read.

Reading Eggs works because it's built on the five pillars for reading success. The program is used in thousands of schools because it's so effective. And kids love it. And you will too as you watch your child make real progress in the most important skill they need for future academic success.

Yours sincerely *Katy Pike*

By the same team that brought you **Mathseeds**

Reading Eggs Reading Skills for First Grade

www.readingeggs.com

ISBN: 978-1-74215-342-1

Copyright © 2018 Blake eLearning
Reprinted 2020

Distributed by:
Blake eLearning
37 West 26th Street
Suite 201. New York, NY 10010

Written by Sara Leman
Publisher: Katy Pike
Editors: Amy Russo and Amanda Santamaria
Design and layout by Modern Art Production Group
Printed by 1010 Printing International LTD

CONTENTS

THE FIVE PILLARS OF READING SUCCESS

Reading Eggs is built on the five components for reading success: phonological and phonemic awareness, phonics, vocabulary, fluency, and comprehension. These proven strategies support learners to achieve reading success.

Phonological and phonemic awareness

Phonological and phonemic awareness are skills we use to hear and play with the individual sounds (phonemes) in words. Skills include breaking words into syllables, blending and segmenting sounds into words, making rhyming words, and using alliteration. Working with word families and playing substitution games help build these skills.

Phonics

Phonics is the relationship between letters and sounds—the correspondence between the sounds in words (phonemes) and the spelling patterns (graphemes) that represent them. Help children develop phonics skills by talking about letters and sounds. For example, *sheep has 3 sounds—sh-ee-p*. These skills help learners decode words for reading and encode sounds for writing and spelling.

sh-ee-p

Vocabulary

Vocabulary is the number of words a child knows and plays an enormous role in the reading process. Build vocabulary by reading books together every day. Discuss new and interesting words and explain what they mean.

Fluency

Fluency is the ability to read a text with accuracy, speed, and expression. One of the best ways to develop fluency is to model good reading when you read aloud. And best of all, reading to your child is proven to be the most important thing you can do to foster a lifelong love of reading.

Comprehension

Comprehension is reading with understanding. A good way to build comprehension skills is to talk about books as you read them together. Ask Who, What, Where, and How questions to discuss what the characters did, what happened and where the story is set.

To find more free tips, printables and ideas, check out the **Reading Eggs** blog at **blog.readingeggs.com**

Reading Eggs Reading Eggs is the fun learn-to-read program that is highly effective, motivating, and easy to integrate into your daily routine.

HOW TO USE THIS BOOK

This book covers lessons 61–120 of the **Reading Eggs** program for First Grade. The program is built on the five pillars of reading success: phonological and phonemic awareness, phonics, vocabulary, fluency, and comprehension.

The year Planner on pages vi-viii provides an overview of the lesson focus in an easy-to-follow, lesson-by-lesson format. If you are using this book alongside the online lessons, we suggest completing the online lesson first before working through the matching workbooks pages.

Lessons

- Each lesson has 4 pages to reinforce learning.

Lesson Review

- At the end of each 4-page lesson, the yellow review panel helps track achievement.

   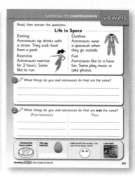

I finished this lesson online.	This egg hatched.	I can identify the vowels. I can read some space words.	I can read
97		◡◡	Life in Space

Color when lesson is complete.

At the end of each online lesson a critter hatches. Write its name here.

Have your learner draw a mouth on the face for each lesson. Are they happy with their learning?

This is the online book title.

Quizzes

- Quizzes test knowledge from the previous five lessons and are followed by a reward certificate.
- Certificates include a checklist to celebrate achievement. These check your learner's understanding of key skills and concepts.

Online Lessons

For a program that is proven to boost reading skills, use this workbook alongside the Reading eggs lessons at **www.readingeggs.com**. The online reading lessons provide a fun and comprehensive program that motivate children to keep learning. Children enjoy the animated lessons, songs and games. By following each online lesson with the matching four lesson pages in this book, children put into practice their new reading skills as well as building essential writing skills.

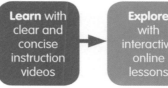

Learn with clear and concise instruction videos → **Explore** with interactive online lessons → **Practice** with workbook lessons

Map 7

Lesson	Lesson Focus	Book Pages	Phonic letters and sounds	Phonically decodable words	High-frequency sight words	Skills
61	the words me, be	2-5			me, be	• Identify the words me and be. • Recognize words for doing actions (verbs). • Read and write using the words me and be and verb.
62	the word families up, ut	6-9	ut, up	cup, pup, cut, up, but, gut, hut, jut, nut, put	three, green	• Read and write words using ut and up. • Recognize the word up.
63	the word families ug, un	10-13	un, ug	bug, dug, hug, jug, mug, rug, tug, bun, sun, fun, gun, pun, run		• Identify the rimes un and ug. • Read and write words using un and ug.
64	the word to	14-17		muck, duck, fluffy, luck, mud, bud	to	• Identify the word to. • Read and write using to. • Review short u words.
65	the word family uck	18-21	uck	fluff, truck, puck, tuck, yuck, stuck		• Read and write words using uck. • Identify rhyming words using uck.
66	the words there, that	22-25		leaf, ant, green, duck, mud, sun	there, that, this, hello	• Identify the sight words there, that, hello, and this. • Recognize the words leaf, mountain, branch, and forest.
67	the word have	26-29		mug, log, cup, green, duck, bug, chin	have	• Identify and read the word have. • Read and write words for facial features and colors.
68	the word they	30-33		leg, dog, cat, sun, run	they	• Identify and read the word they. • Read and write words for body parts and numbers.
69	the word do	34-37		jump, run	do, can, cannot	• Identify and read the word do. • Read and write using verbs.
70	Review	38-41	us	bus, bug, bun, cab, cup, cut, duck, hot, jog, muck, nun, not, pup, rug, run, slug, sun		• Read and write words using the short /u/ sound. • Recognize known verbs and sight words.
Map 7 Quiz	Revision	42-45				

Map 8

Lesson	Lesson Focus	Book Pages	Phonic letters and sounds	Phonically decodable words	High-frequency sight words	Skills
71	the words my, come, play	46-49		band	come, my, here, goes, day, play	• Identify the words my, come, play, goes. • Read and write words from a party theme.
72	the word families ed, eg	50-53	ed, eg, ing	bed, red, leg, peg, beg, egg	baby, open, hello	• Read and write ed and eg words. • Recognize verbs ending with ing.
73	the word families et, ed	54-57	ed, et	bed, fed, wed, red, led, ted, pet, net, jet, vet, wet, hen, ten, pen, leg, egg		• Read and write et and ed words. • Recognize the days of the week.
74	the word families eg, et	58-61	eg, et	pet, bet, get, jet, met, set, vet, wet, yet, den, pen, hen, ten, when, men, zen	where	• Read and write eg and et words. • Recognize words for pets.
75	the words where, word family un	62-65		pen, ten, peg, men, hen, shop	where, when, down, up, go, now	• Identify and read the words where and when. • Read and write en words.
76	the word family en, eg	66-69	eg	leg, beg, keg, peg, peck		• Identify the rimes eg and en. • Read and write words from short e word families.
77	the words who, lives	70-73		peck, shell	who, lives, here, into	• Identify and read the words who, lives, and here. • Read and write animal words.
78	the word what	74-77		wing, tail, log, bed, net, her	what	• Identify and read the word what. • Read and write words from a dragon theme.
79	the word family ell	78-81	ell	bell, tell, yell, fell, well, shell, sell, hell	who, what, where	• Read and write words with the rime ell. • Identify the words when, who, what, where.
80	Review	82-85		egg, net, bed, red, jet, peg, ten, pen	seven	• Revise all known word families. • Read and write words in a birthday party theme.
Map 8 Quiz	Revision	86-87				

Map 9

Lesson	Lesson Focus	Book Pages	Phonic letters and sounds	Phonically decodable words	High-frequency sight words	Skills
81	the word with	90-93	short vowels	pen, pig, leg, log, mug, mop, hat, hug, bed, box	have, with, what, you	• Revise consonant-vowel-consonant words. • Read and write using the word with. • Recognize and read words associated with the five senses.
82	the word family ie	94-97	ie, ile	pie, tie, lie, smile, crocodile	going, where, want	• Identify the sound ie as in pie and smile. • Recognize and read the word want.
83	the word family i-e	98-101	ie, ine, ike	lie, line, mine, like, hike	shoe, car, table	• Identify the split digraph i-e as in line. • Read and write the word help.
84	the word family ine	102-105	ine, ide, ike	dine, pine, fine, spine, shrine	too, off, over, this	• Identify the rime ine. • Sort words that contain ie or i_e.
85	the word family sh	106-109	sh	shell, shop, sheep, ship, shed	shop, bike	• Identify the sound sh. • Read and write sh words.
86	the word family sh	110-113	sh	shelley, sheep, shop, shopping	buy, tried, these, new	• Review the sound sh. • Read and write sh words.
87	the word family i-e	114-117	long i	kite, bite, bike, hike, hide, ride	white, nine, girl, boy	• Identify the rimes that can be made with i_e. • Read and write i_e words.
88	the word family ch	118-121	ch	chat, chick, cheese, chin, chips, chest	says, ask, why	• Identify the sound ch. • Read and write ch words.
89	the word family th	122-125	th	throw, thanks, thin, that, thud, thick, thorn, think	none, two, stayed, home	• Identify the sound th. • Read and write th words.
90	Review	126-129	ch	chimp, chicken, cheese, chilli	these, made, together	• Review the sounds ie, sh, ch, and th. • Read and write ch words.
Map 9 Quiz	Revision	130-131				

Map 10

Lesson	Lesson Focus	Book Pages	Phonic letters and sounds	Phonically decodable words	High-frequency sight words	Skills
91	the soft c word family	134-137	soft c	city, celery, cement, bicycle, park, shark, dark, bark	one, two, three, four, five	• Identify words with the soft c sound. • Recognize when the soft c sound applies. • Read and write words with the soft c sound.
92	the word family ice	138-141	ice	mice, rice, dice, slice, line, bike, nine, fine, lime, vine	fly, look, white, fine, nine	• Identify the rime ice. • Read and write ice words. • Revise other i_e word families. • Make compound words.
93	the soft g word family	142-145	soft g	cage, page, sage, stage, rage	today, park, Saturday	• Identify words with the soft g sound. • Recognize when the soft g sound applies. • Read and write words with the soft g sound.
94	the word family ake	146-149	ake	cake, lake, rake, bake, take, snake, shake, make, wake	snake, giraffe, wheel, shark	• Identify the split digraph a_e. • Read and write words ending with ake.
95	the word family a_e	150-153	long a, ane	cane, mane, lane, plane, cage, ape, game	flew, bowl, brother, everywhere, what, about, another	• Identify the rimes that can be made with a_e. • Read and write a_e words.
96	the word family ace	154-157	ace	space, lace, face	clouds, sky, stars, above	• Identify the rime ace. • Read and write ace words. • Revise other a_e word families.
97	vowels	158-161	vowels	life, space	hours, outside, white, purple, yellow, orange	• Identify the vowel letters. • Learn space theme words. • Read and write compound words.
98	the vowel word familes	162-165	long vowel words	make, snake, five, ape	these, out, eight, blue	• Identify the long and short vowel sounds. • Read and write with craft theme words. • Learn the word eight.
99	the word family ending y	166-169	y on the end	itchy, hairy, floppy, rusty, party, creepy	sleep, party, work, easy, flew, plane, high	• Review the sound ee. • Use the letter y as a word ending. • Read and write words that end with y.
100	Review	170-173		five, mice, cage	up, down, night, day, in, out, five, nine, eight	• Review the sounds i_e, a_e and y on the end of a word. • Recognize sight words and theme words.
Map 10 Quiz	Revision	174-175				

Map 11

YEAR PLANNER

Lesson	Lesson Focus	Book Pages	Phonic letters and sounds	Phonically decodable words	High-frequency sight words	Skills
101	the word family oo (short)	178-181	oo	cook, book, wool, foot, look, took	dressed, chocolate, delicious, excited, second, loved	• Identify the short oo sound, as in book. • Read and write short oo words.
102	the word family oo (long)	182-185	oo	roof, zoo, noon, moon, cool, spoon, baboon, cockatoo, kangaroo	said, here, took, who, school	• Identify the long oo sound, as in soon. • Read and write long oo words.
103	the word family ole	186-189	ole	pole, sole, mole, hole, stole, woke, poke, joke, bone, stone, cone	dark, down, ground, own, phone, stopped	• Identify the rime ole. • Read and write words ending with ole.
104	the word family o_e	190-193	long o, e sounds	rode, code, vote, rose, boat, coat, goat, float, tadpole, flagpole, foam	behind, bubbly, suddenly, together, around, through, they	• Identify the rimes that can be made with o_e. • Read and write o_e words. • Make compound words.
105	blends	194-197	blends	frog, clam, slam, swam, grub, crab, plug, grab, slug, shell	phone, friends, open, eat	• Identify blends. • Read and write words with blends.
106	more blends	198-201	blends	crab, clam, frog, fly, green, trunk, lunch, crash, tree, grotty	crash, hungry, green, happy, blue, lunch	• Identify more blends. • Read and write words with blends.
107	the word family ea	202-205	ea	pea, seal, leaf, dream, peach, beach, beast, eat, peace	down, sitting, eating, scary, looking, lovely	• Recognize that the digraph ea makes the sound /ee/. • Read and write ea words. • Identify words which have opposite meanings.
108	the word family u_e	206-209	long u words	cube, flute, tune, duke, June, tube	worried, perfect, choose, tongue, blue,	• Identify the rimes that can be made with u_e. • Read and write u_e words.
109	the word family er	210-213	er	helper, cleaner, badger, leaky, gardener, hotter, plumber	anything, better, sister, brother, bigger, garden, house	• Identify the word ending er. • Read and write words that end with er. • Add er to name occupations.
110	blends	214-217	blends	strong, crunchy, glossy, ground, cloud, squishy, weak	flower, white, brown, cloud, drank, dry, pretty, adjective	• Review initial blends. • Recognize and use adjectives.
Map 11 Quiz	Revision	218-219				

Map 12

Lesson	Lesson Focus	Book Pages	Phonic letters and sounds	Phonically decodable words	High-frequency sight words	Skills
111	blends	222-225	blends	track, crack, back, snack, trip, crashed, stuck, truck	happy, wanted, three, why, cry, happy, friends	• Review initial blends. • Read and write words using blends.
112	syllables	226-229	syllables	exercise, drink, growing, beetle	water, food, clothes, eaten, keeping, sunlight, somewhere	• Identify syllables in words. • Recognize that syllables align with vowels. • Read and write words about keeping healthy.
113	end blends	230-233	end blends	milk, stinky, sink, pink, drink, skunk, stamp, thump, rabbit, duckling	wanted, running, wants, spider, keeping	• Identify end blends. • Read and write words with blends.
114	the word family oa	234-237	oa	oats, coast, road, toast, float, goat, raincoat	picture, thunderstorm, house, flowers	• Identify the sound oa. • Read and write oa words. • Make compound words.
115	the word family ir	238-241	ir	dirt, shirt, skirt, sunlight, seedling, warm, leaf	warm, water, soil, grow, need, live	• Identify the sound made with a vowel and r as /ir/. • Recognize the combinations that make /ir/ – ar, er, ir, or, ur. • Read and write words with /ir/ sounds.
116	the word family igh	242-245	igh	night, bright, sight, high, sigh, moonlight, sandpaper, ice cube	family, forest, caring, goodnight, right, day, try	• Identify the letters igh making the long i sound. • Recognize words that contain igh. • Read and write igh words.
117	nouns	246-249	nouns	raincoat, waterfall, bathroom, coast, toast	shirt, wanted, loudly, chewed, caught, night, friends, better	• Identify nouns and proper nouns. • Recognize that proper nouns need capital letters. • Read and write nouns and proper nouns.
118	the word family or	250-253	or	score, wore, store, shore, boots, jumper, coat, popcorn, knight, horse	weather, cloudy, sunny, windy, snow, sunny, rainy	• Identify different spellings for the sound /or/. • Read and write /or/ words. • Recognize clothing and weather words.
119	verbs	254-257	verbs	imagine, insect, squeal, cling, creep, swoop, scuttle, sideways, flap	girl, open, closed, clothes, remember, whistle, scared	• Identify verbs as doing or action words. • Recognize that almost every sentence has a verb. • Read and write verbs.
120	the word family ay	258-261	ay	boat, pink, store, bird, truck, goat, crab, cling, feet, crabs, stay, okay, today	apple, library, eight, spelling, their, walk	• Identify the sound ay. • Read and write ay words.
Map 12 Quiz	Revision	262-263				

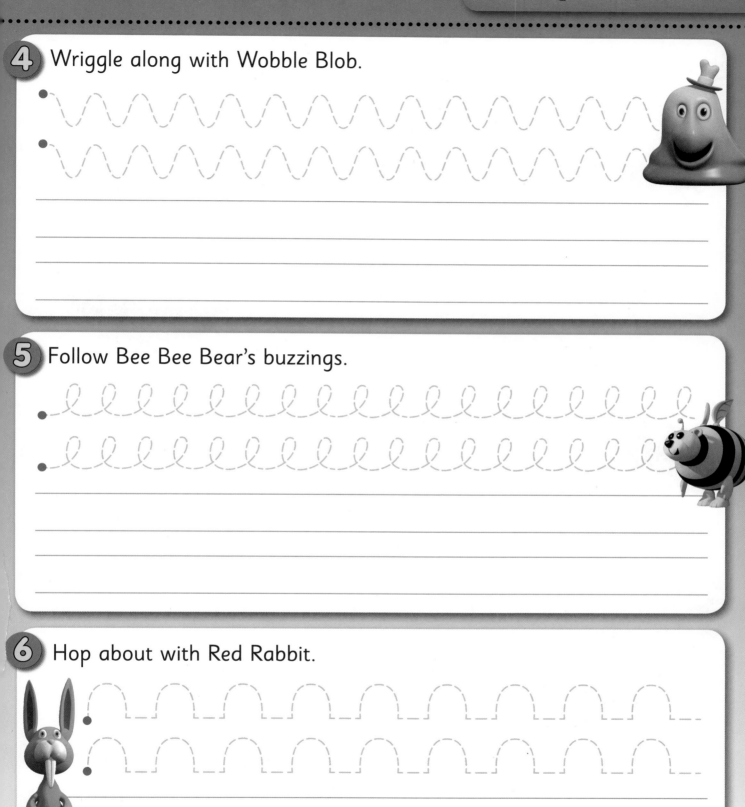

4 Wriggle along with Wobble Blob.

5 Follow Bee Bee Bear's buzzings.

6 Hop about with Red Rabbit.

1 ✏️ Complete the alphabet snakes.

2 ✏️ Draw lines to match.

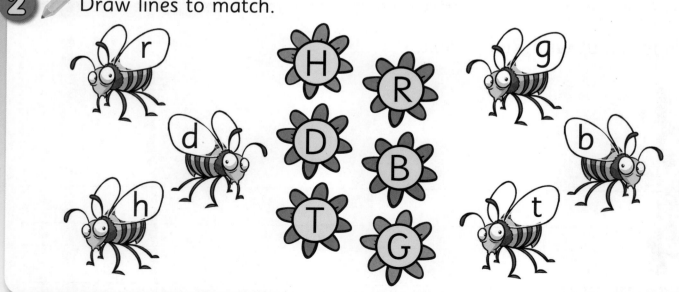

Reading eggs First Grade Workbook

1 Say the word. ✏️ Write the beginning sound.

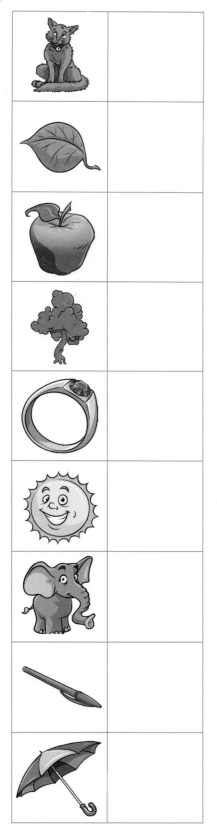

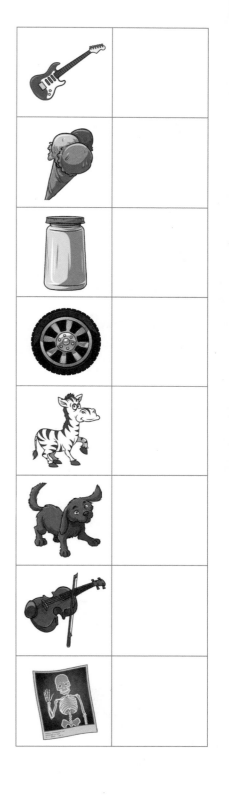

1 How many syllables?

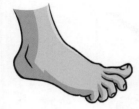

| 1 | 2 | 3 |

| 1 | 2 | 3 |

| 1 | 2 | 3 |

| 1 | 2 | 3 |

| 2 | 3 | 4 |

| 1 | 2 | 3 |

| 1 | 2 | 3 |

| 2 | 3 | 4 |

2 How many sounds?

| 2 | 3 | 4 |

| 2 | 3 | 4 |

| 2 | 3 | 4 |

| 2 | 3 | 4 |

| 2 | 3 | 4 |

| 2 | 3 | 4 |

| 2 | 3 | 4 |

| 2 | 3 | 4 |

Reading eggs First Grade Workbook

1 Circle the correct word.

dig
dog

box
six

fun
fin

leg
log

tip
top

mop
met

ant
and

ten
tan

log
lot

hill
hit

pin
pan

shop
top

1 ✏️ Write the missing letter.

h____n

s____n

d____g

h____p

w____b

b____t

b____x

m____g

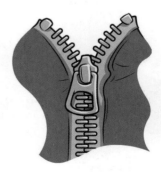

z____p

1 ✏️ Write each word. Color the star if you know the word.

see ☆	have ☆	at ☆
the ☆	he ☆	and ☆
I ☆	she ☆	can ☆
is ☆	was ☆	good ☆
this ☆	has ☆	you ☆
look ☆	said ☆	are ☆
go ☆	little ☆	am ☆
by ☆	like ☆	in ☆

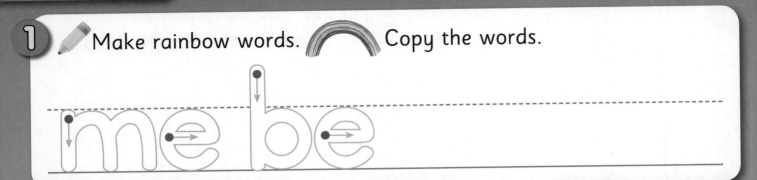

me be

1 ✏️ Make rainbow words. 🌈 Copy the words.

m e b e

2 Color the correct word. ✗ Cross out the wrong word.

Look at [me] [be] .

Can this [me] [be] a hat?

I can [me] [be] silly.

Look at [me] [be] draw.

3 Color the path of **me** words to Me Be Fish.

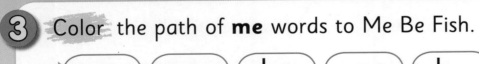

→ me	me	be	we	he	be	we
be	me	me	be	we	be	he
we	be	me	me	me	he	we
he	we	be	he	me	me	me

me be

1 ✏️ Complete the sentences.

| me | We | be |

Look! _____ can see a cat.

Tom the Dog will _____ here soon.

Meg the Hen gave _____ an egg.

2 Complete the sentence and ✏️ draw a picture.

Look at _____ run!

3 ✏️ Write the word in a box.

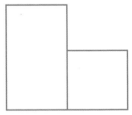

me   be

1 ✏️ Join each word to a picture.

climb

eat

laugh

draw

read

sleep

2 ✏️ Write your own sentence. Draw a picture.

I can

me be

Read, then answer the questions.

Fox or tree?

I am Ben. Look at me!
I can be a tree.
Look at Tess.
She can be a fox.

1. Ben can be a _____ .

   a bee   **b** tree   **c** fox

2. He is a _____ .

   a fox   **b** girl   **c** boy

3. Tess can be a _____ .

   a hat   **b** fox   **c** tree

1 🖉 Join each word to a picture.

nut

cut

hut

cup

pup

log

2 Color the **ut** words **red** and the **up** words **blue**.

nutty	less	puppy	silly
zipper	cut	happy	supper
puppy	messy	gutter	but
shut	pup	hut	hiccup
bug	put	cup	bat

Reading **eggs** First Grade Workbook

1 ✏️ Complete.

Read	Write	Color
hut		
cut		
nut		

2 Color the word that matches the picture.

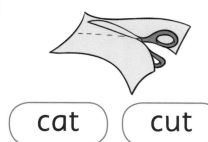      

| cat | cut | | but | cup | | pup | pip |

3 ✏️ Write two

ut words	**up** words
 _____	_____
_____	_____

1 Use the words in the box to complete the sentences.

three six ten green red blue

Look at the _____ , _____ cups.

Look at the _____ , _____ frogs.

Look at the _____ , _____ socks.

2 Draw a red cup.

Draw three nuts.

3 Circle the rhyming words in each row.

| nut | rat | but | pet | hut | cut |

| pop | cup | tap | pup | up | lip |

| put | set | hit | met | net | pet |

Read, then answer the questions.

Puppy and bluebird

Look at the puppy.
The puppy is happy.
The puppy can see a bluebird.
Bluebird can go up, up, up.

1 The puppy is _____ .

a sad   **b** happy   **c** silly

2 What can the puppy see? _____

a a bird   **b** a frog   **c** a puppy

3 The bird is _____ .

a red   **b** green   **c** blue

I finished this lesson online.	This egg hatched.	I know the sounds: up and ut.	I can read

1 🖊 Join each word to a picture.

rug

run

bug

bun

sun

mug

2 Color the **ug** words **red** and the **un** words **blue**.

rug	mug	bat	hug
fun	ten	sun	bun
bug	tug	dug	cab

3 🖊 Complete each word family.

jug

m _____

b _____

sun

f _____

b _____

Reading **eggs** First Grade Workbook

1 ✏️ Use the words in the box to complete the sentences.

| run | it | skip | tag |

"I can _____," said Sam.

"I can run and _____," said Jazz.

"You are _____, Sid!" said Jazz.

"I can _____," said Sid.

2 ✏️ Unjumble the words and label each picture.

g r u _____

n u s _____

n b u _____

g u b _____

g m u _____

g j u _____

1 ✏️ Write each word.

 _____

 _____

 _____

 _____

2 Match the jigsaw pieces to label the pictures.

s	ag
pl	ip
sk	ug
t	un

 _____

 _____

 _____

3 ✏️ Write the word in a box.

rug   jug   skip

Read, then answer the questions.

Little Bug

Can you see the little bug?
The bug can run and skip.
He has lots of fun.
He plays on a rug in the sun.

① The bug is _____ .
a big   **b** little   **c** sad

② He can run and _____ .
a skip   **b** hop   **c** go

③ Does this bug have fun? _____
a yes   **b** no

④ Where does he play? _____
a in a jug   **b** on a rug   **c** on a mug

1 ✏️ Make a rainbow word. 🌈 Copy the word.

_____

✝🅾

_____

2 (Circle) **to**.

Jazz has the ball. She gives it to Sam. He throws it to Sid. Sid rolls it to Tom.

....

Who has the ball now? _____

3 Find the words. Color them.

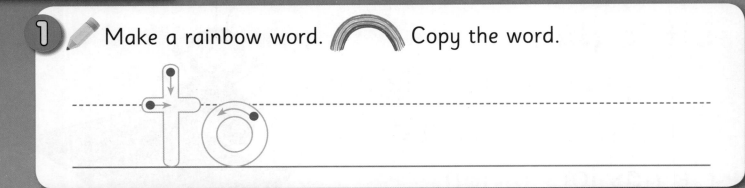

a	r	e	a	j	e	r	y	o	u	b	t	c
h	i	s	x	t	h	e	d	k	s	a	i	d
q	b	e	e	l	s	t	o	t	x	o	m	e
v	e	r	y	f	m	n	w	e	s	r	v	b
i	v	h	e	r	u	e	h	y	p	n	o	t

to

1 Complete each sentence with a word from the box.

puppy   sun   duck

Gus is a

‒‒‒‒‒‒‒‒‒‒‒‒‒‒‒‒‒‒‒‒‒‒‒‒‒‒‒‒‒

_____ .

Tubs is a

‒‒‒‒‒‒‒‒‒‒‒‒‒‒‒‒‒‒‒‒‒‒‒‒‒‒‒‒‒

_____ .

Tubs runs in the

‒‒‒‒‒‒‒‒‒‒‒‒‒‒‒‒‒‒‒‒‒‒‒‒‒‒‒‒‒

_____ .

2 Color the correct word.

Tubs runs ⬚so⬚ ⬚to⬚ the mud.

Gus is ⬚in⬚ ⬚of⬚ the mud.

Poor Tubs ⬚in⬚ ⬚is⬚ stuck in the mud.

1 ✏️ Label the picture.   puppy   duck   mud

2 ✏️ Read the questions and (circle) the answers.

Is Gus a duck?	**Yes No**
Is Tubs a puppy?	**Yes No**
Is the puppy muddy?	**Yes No**
Is the duck muddy?	**Yes No**
Is the duck stuck?	**Yes No**
Is the puppy stuck?	**Yes No**
Is it fun to be in the mud?	**Yes No**
Does the duck run in the sun?	**Yes No**
Does the pup run in the sun?	**Yes No**

Reading **eggs** First Grade Workbook

1 Help Smile do his washing. Color the path of **to** words.

to	to	he	we
if	to	to	of
we	in	to	at
he	is	to	to

2 Trace and write the words.

to   in

3 Use the words to complete the sentences.

Sam runs _____ his pup.

He is stuck _____ mud.

The pup likes _____ be in the mud.

I finished this lesson online.	This egg hatched.	I can read and write the word: to.	I can read
 64			The muddy puppy

1 Join each word to a picture.

duck

muck

luck

stuck

truck

yuck

2 Join the jigsaw pieces. Write each word.

m

d

l

st

u c k

_____

_____

_____

_____

uck

1 Color the right word. ✗ Cross out the wrong word.

truck

duck

muck

mug

puppy

yummy

duck

stuck

2 ✏ Draw

a fluffy duck.

a dog on a log.

3 Circle the rhyming words.

dog   bog   duck   log   Tom   fog

1 ✏️ Put the words in order to make each sentence.

> duck muck.
> stuck in
> Fluff the
> the gets

_____

_____

_____

_____

> dog the
> logs. gets
> lots of
> Tom

_____

_____

_____

_____

2 ✏️ Complete the sentences using these words.

> in got mud truck see

Fluff got stuck in the _____.

Tom can _____ the bog.

He _____ lots of logs.

Fluff was _____ luck!

She can drive the _____.

uck

Read, then answer the questions.

My Puppy

This is my little puppy.
He is very funny.
He likes to play in the mud.
The mud is good!

1 This is my _____ puppy.
a big   b little   c happy

2 My puppy is _____ .
a sad   b fluffy   c funny

3 Where does my puppy play? _____
a mud   b tree   c sun

4 How is the mud? _____
a bad   b hot   c good

| I finished this lesson online. | This egg hatched. | I know the word family: uck. | I can read |

Fluff the duck

1 🖊 Trace and write the words.

there

that

this

2 Circle the matching words in each row.

there	what	when	there
this	those	this	the
that	than	thin	that

3 Color there = **red**, this = **yellow**, that = **green**.

that	this	there	this
there	that	this	that

**that
there**

1 Crack the code!

e = ❀
h = ▲
a = ✓
t = ★
s = ●
r = ■
i = ✹
w = ☾

▲ ❀ ■ ❀

★ ▲ ✹ ●
_____

_____

★ ▲ ✓ ★

★ ▲ ❀
_____

_____

☾ ✓ ●

★ ▲ ❀ ■ ❀
_____

_____

2 Circle the words.

there   this   that

This is Sid and Sam. They see
Jazz. She is up there in a tree.
Come down from that tree, Jazz!

3 ✏ Write the word in a box.

there   this   that

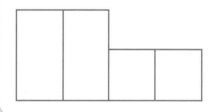
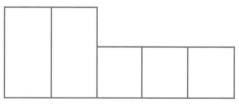
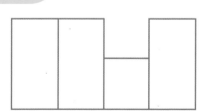

1 Join each word to a picture.

mountain

forest

tree

branch

leaf

ant

2 Put the words in order to make a sentence.

forest. big a was There

----

that
there

This is a fact book about ants.

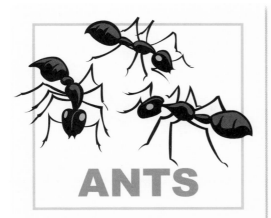

Contents	Page
Chapter 1	
Kinds of ants	1
Chapter 2	
What ants eat	5
Chapter 3	
Where ants live	7

Answer the questions.

1. What is this book about? _____

....

2. How many chapters are there? _____

....

3. What will page 7 tell you?

_____

....

4. What is Chapter 2 about?

_____

I finished this lesson online.	This egg hatched.	I can read and write the words: there and that.	I can read
			Mountain top

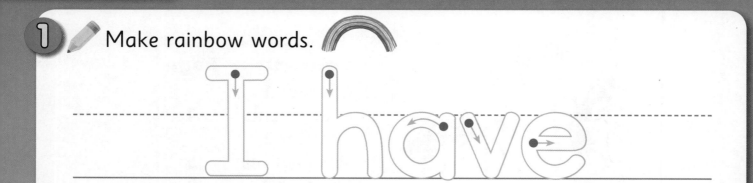

1 ✏️ Make rainbow words. 🌈

I have

2 Join the letters to make **have**.

h	d	i	p
u	a	o	n
k	x	v	e
c	s	w	p

3 Find **have**.

hat	have	have
hat	**are**	has
here	have	**his**
who	now	have

4 Color **yes** or **no**.

I **have** one eye. (yes) (no)

I **have** ten legs. (yes) (no)

I **have** one tooth. (yes) (no)

I **have** blue hair. (yes) (no)

have

1 ✏️ Write the labels.

eye   nose   chin   ear   hair   mouth

2 ✏️ Complete the sentence.

2   He has _____

have

1 ✏ Draw a picture of your face. Label your:
- eyes
- ears
- nose
- mouth
- hair

2 Complete these sentences about you.

> red   black   brown   yellow
> blue   green   pink

My hair is _____.

My eyes are _____.

3 Complete.

Dan's puppy has two _____.

She has _____ fur.

She has a pink _____.

have

Read, then answer the questions.

Eyes

We have two eyes.
They help us to see.
Some eyes are brown.
Some eyes are green.
Some are blue.

1 What is this text about?

a eggs   **b** eyes   **c** ears

2 Circle true or false?

a All boys have blue eyes.   True   False
b All girls have green eyes.   True   False
c Some eyes are brown.   True   False

3 What color eyes do you have?

_____

I finished this lesson online.	This egg hatched.	I can read and write the word: have.	I can read

1 ✏️ Make a rainbow word. Copy the word.

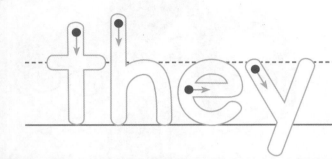

2 Join the letters to make **they**.

t	n	o	a
s	h	v	y
b	p	e	r
f	c	w	u

3 Circle **they**.

they	that	the
her	**hat**	they
to	they	**then**
they	have	that

4 Make words with these letters.

2-letter word: ⚪ ⚪

3-letter word: ⚪ ⚪ ⚪

4-letter word: ⚪ ⚪ ⚪ ⚪

they

1 ✏ Trace and write the words.

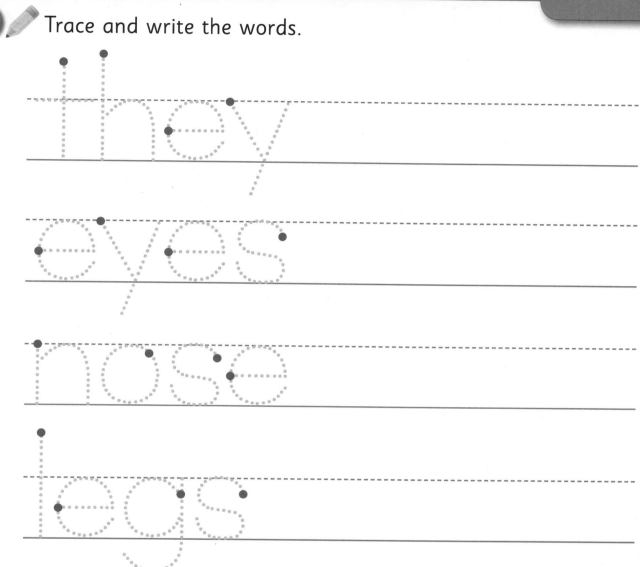

they

eyes

nose

legs

2 ✏ Use the words to complete the sentences.

Cats and dogs have four _____.

They have two _____.

They have one _____.

_____ both have two ears.

1 Read the labels. Color the animals.

orange

black

green

black

yellow

pink

brown

blue

white

gray

2 ✏️ Write four sentences about these animals.

This cat _____.

This dog _____.

They _____.

They _____.

they

Answer the questions.

Dogs and cats

1 How are dogs and cats the same?

_____

_____

_____

2 How are dogs and cats **not** the same?

_____

_____

_____

3 Do you like dogs or cats? Why?

_____

_____

I finished this lesson online.	This egg hatched.	I can read and write the word: they.	I can read
68			

do

1 ✏️ Make a rainbow word. 🌈 Trace and copy.

2 Follow the path of **do** words to get Gus the dump truck to his job.

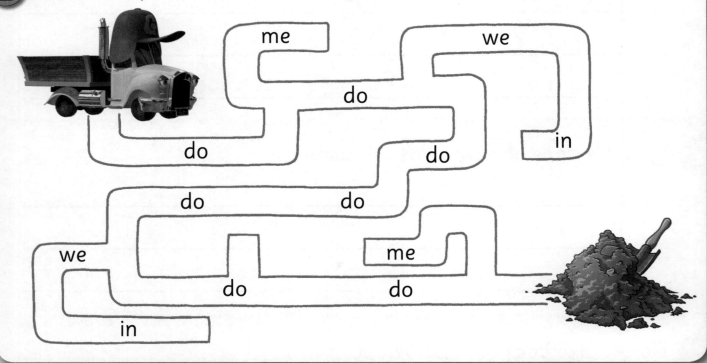

3 Add **Do** and answer the questions.

_____ you like bugs?   **Yes   No**

_____ you run fast?   **Yes   No**

_____ you eat apples?   **Yes   No**

do

1 Join each picture to a word.

jump

swim

fly

grin

skip

run

2 Color the **verbs** – the doing words.

run	bug	blue	dog	swim
cat	we	jump	one	green
I	skip	sun	fly	grin

3 What can **you** do?

I can _____ .

I can _____ .

I can _____ .

1 ✏️ Complete each sentence with a word from the box.

| jump swim run |

Fluff the duck can _____.

Frogfish can _____.

Tom the dog can _____.

2 Color the correct word. ✗ Cross out the wrong one.

Sam the ant (can) (cannot) fly.

Frogfish (can) (cannot) jump.

Fluff the duck (can) (cannot) swim.

Tom the dog (can) (cannot) buzz.

3 What do you think Jet Set can do? Complete.

He can _____.

He cannot _____.

do

Read, then answer the questions.

Things they can do

Sam the ant can run and jump.
Zee the bee cannot swim. But she
can buzz. Bee Bee Bear cannot
jog but he can fly.

1 What can Sam the ant do?
a buzz and fly   **b** run and jump   **c** jog

2 Who can buzz?
a Sam   **b** Bee Bee Bear   **c** Zee the Bee

3 Yes or no? Bee Bee Bear cannot jog.
a yes   **b** no

4 Who cannot swim?
a Sam   **b** Zee the bee   **c** Bee Bee Bear

5 Can you swim? _____ .

I finished this lesson online.	This egg hatched.	I can read and write the word: do.	I can read

1 Color .

ut ◄ ug ◄ up ◄ un ◄ uck ◄

2 Sort the words into their word families.

ut	ug	up	un	uck

3 Write the word in a box.

bug rug pup fun

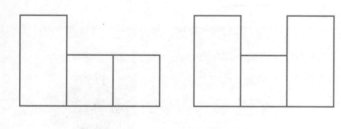
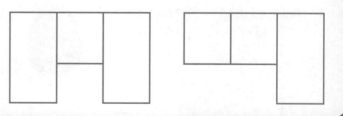

Reading eggs First Grade Workbook

1 Complete each sentence using a word from the box.

| They　The　that　This　have |

I _____ two bugs.

_____ are green.

_____ is a cat.

_____ cat is black.

Look at _____ black cat!

2 Read and answer.

What color are the bugs? _____

What color is the cat? _____

3 Color the correct word. ✗ Cross out the wrong word.

Do To you run?

Look at me be .

We can go to do the park.

I will me be there!

1 (Circle) the **uck** words.

jump	muck	bug	truck
run	cup	luck	stuck
skip	duck	mud	look

2 Say the name of each picture. Color the word ending.

(up) (ub) (ut) (uck) (un) (ug) (uck) (ub)

3 Complete the word chain. Use a different letter each time.

but • ____ut • ____ut • ____ut

4 (Circle) the words that rhyme.

 sun   man   fun   rug   sat   run

 cup   sup   mop   pup   hip   cap

 tub   pot   cub   top   rub   dog

1 Join each picture to a word.

jump

run

fly

skip

2 ✏ Write a sentence using these words.

dog   legs   muddy

_____

_____

3 ✏ Read and draw.

A dog has four legs.	A cat has two eyes.

I finished this lesson online.	This egg hatched.	I know the word families: up, ut, ug, un, ub, and uck.	I can read
 (70)			

1 Say the name of each picture. Color the word family.

(ug) (uck)

(ub) (ug)

(up) (ut)

(ay) (ee)

2 Circle the rhyming words in each row.

hut	mat	hen	cut	put	but
fan	fun	sun	hat	pip	run
hub	rat	tub	dog	rub	cub

3 Color the correct word. ✗ Cross out the wrong word.

This is [me] [be].

She can [me] [be] funny.

4 Read and draw.

This is one leaf.	There are three bugs.

MAP 7 LESSONS 61 TO 70

Quiz

5 ✏ Complete each sentence.

to do have They

I _____ two brown eyes.

_____ run and jump.

What can you _____ ?

Tubs ran _____ the mud.

6 Look at the picture. ✔ Check the matching sentence.
✘ Cross out the wrong sentence.

☐ Fluffy the duck can drive her truck.

☐ Here is a mountain.

☐ On the top of that leaf there was an ant.

7 Make words with these letters. e t e h r

2-letter word: ◯ ◯

3-letter word: ◯ ◯ ◯

5-letter word: ◯ ◯ ◯ ◯ ◯

FANTASTIC!

YOU COMPLETED ★

MAP 7

YOU CAN:

☐ Recognize the: **up, ut, ug, un, ub,** and **uck** word families.

☐ Read and write the words: **me, be, too, there, that, have, they,** and **do**.

☐ Read other words such as: **look, sleep, drive, jump, fly, run, leg, ear, eye, nose, leaf, mountain, puppy, muddy,** and **green**.

☐ Read lots of sentences:
Tom the dog gets lots of logs.

☐ Read these books:

Balloons go up

Fluff the duck

Dogs and cats

Run and jump

1 Find your treasure.

ten bugs, six ducks,
three trucks, a mug, a sun,
a pup, five red flowers,
four blue flowers,
two yellow flowers

1 ✏️ Trace and write.

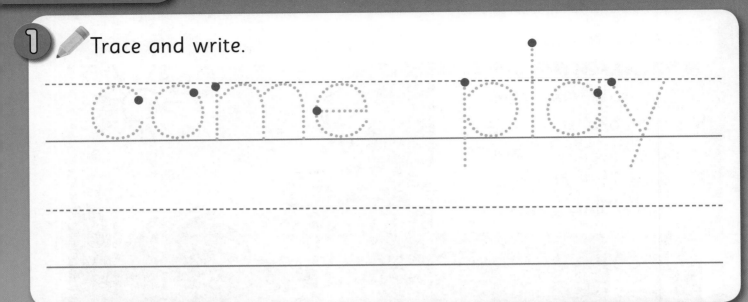

come play

2 Label Nutty Newt's things.   my

This is _____ scarf.

This is _____ hat.

This is _____ sock.

This is _____ bag.

This is _____ shoe.

3 (Circle) the correct word. ✗ Cross out the wrong word.

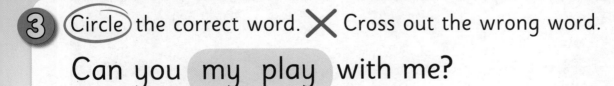

Can you   my play   with me?

Here   there come   my dogs.

Where is   him my   bag.

Reading **eggs** First Grade Workbook

my come play

1 ✏️ Join each word to a picture.

table

chair

plate

food

band

people

2 (Circle) the correct word. ✖ Cross out the wrong word.

Put the money on the puppy table .

I like to eat muddy party food.

Sit on this chair people .

I can hear the band playing songs .

3 ✏️ Write the word in a box.   goes plate food

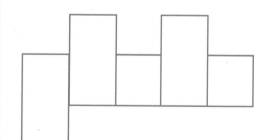
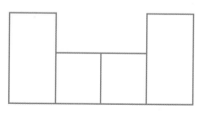
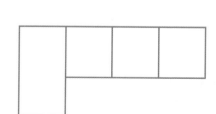

1. Finish each sentence. Draw a picture.

band   goes   my   comes   plays   people

The boy _____ to a party.

The dog _____ at the park.

Here _____ the bus.

I like _____ cat.

They can see the _____ .

The man plays in the _____ .

my come play

Read, then answer the questions.

Come to my Picnic!

Jazz the cat is having a picnic party.
When: Sunday, May 10
Where: the park
Time: 2–4
You will need: a hat, a cup, a plate, a mat to sit on.
Come and play!

1 Who is having a picnic party?
a Sam **b** Jazz **c** Sid

2 When is it?
a Sunday **b** Saturday **c** Friday

3 Where is it?
a the forest **b** the pool **c** the park

4 Write 3 things you will need.

_____

_____

5 Write 2 things you like to do at a picnic.

_____

I finished this lesson online.	This egg hatched.	I can read and write the words: my, come, and play.	I can read
 71			

ed eg

1 Color the **ed** words **red** and the **eg** words **blue**.

| bed | red | leg | peg |
| fed | Meg | led | bed |

2 Sort the words into their word families.

ed   **eg**

_____   _____

_____   _____

_____   _____

_____   _____

3 Label the pictures. Color the odd one out.

| | | |

4 Write the word in a box.

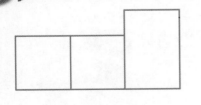 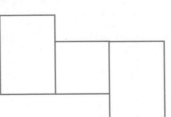 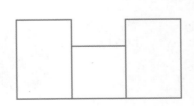

fed
red
beg

1 Join each word to a picture.

bed

baby

cracking

dinosaur

nest

leg

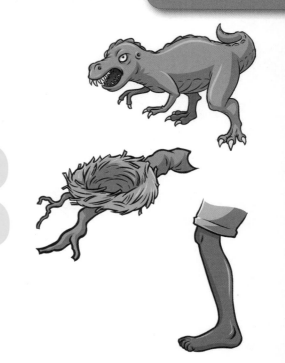

2 Put the words through the machine. Write the new words.

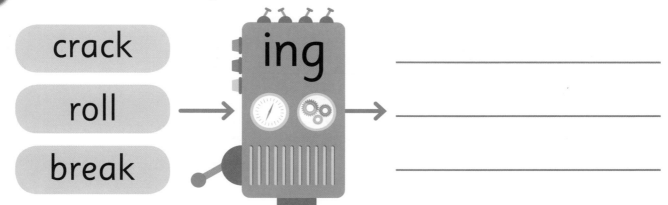

crack

roll

break

ing

_____

_____

_____

3 Complete the sentences.

The dinosaur egg is _____ .

The dinosaur egg is _____ .

1 Match to the correct picture.

This is a dinosaur egg.

The egg is cracking.

This is a dinosaur.

2 Put the words in the correct order. Write each sentence.

green I egg. see a can

_____

a dinosaur It egg. is

_____

rolling? Can it you see

_____

egg dinosaur The cracking. is

_____

Read, then answer the questions.

Crack!

The red dinosaur sits in her nest.
She lays a green egg.
The egg gets hot in the sun.
Crack! Crack! Crack! The egg breaks.

1 What is the story about?
a a bird   **b** a dinosaur egg   **c** a sunny day

2 What color is the dinosaur?
a green   **b** yellow   **c** red

3 How many eggs are there?
a one   **b** two   **c** three

4 What do you think
is inside the egg?
Draw a picture.

I finished this lesson online.

This egg hatched.

I can read and write: eg and ed words.

I can read

The dinosaur egg

1 Use the word wheel to make a list of **et** words.

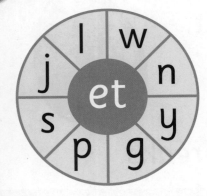

_____ _____

_____ _____

_____ _____

2 (Circle) the rhyming words in each row.

| egg | met | leg | red | beg |

| fed | jet | peg | bet | vet |

| bed | wed | pet | led | ten |

3 Color the sound you hear at the end of the word.

d   t   g

d   t   g

d   t   g

d   t   g

d   t   g

d   t   g

et ed

1 Join each word to a picture.

book

egg

ten

bell

hen

pen

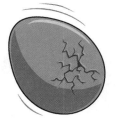

2 Find the matching pairs.

Wednesday

Tuesday

Friday

Monday

Saturday

Sunday

Monday

Thursday

Friday

Tuesday

Wednesday

Sunday

Saturday

Thursday

3 How many days in a week? _____

1 Use this calendar to answer the questions.

 THIS WEEK

Monday

Tuesday

Wednesday

Thursday

Friday

Saturday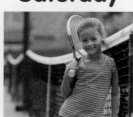

Sunday

On which day did this happen?

 _____

 _____

 _____

 _____

 _____

 _____

 _____

2 What do you do on

Monday? _____   Saturday? _____

et ed

1 Match each sentence to a picture.

On Monday,
Meg the hen lays ten eggs.

On Tuesday,
Meg looks at a book.

On Wednesday,
Meg gets ten little, red beds.

On Thursday,
Meg gets ten red pens.

On Friday,
Meg gets ten little bells.

2 Finish these sentences.

On Saturday, _____
_____.

On Sunday, _____
_____.

I finished this lesson online.	This egg hatched.	I can read and write: et and ed words, and recognize the days of the week.	I can read
 73			Meg the hen

1 Use the wheels to make words. 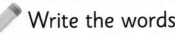 Write the words.

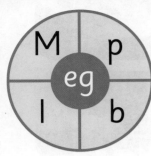

eg _____

_____

_____

_____

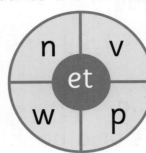

et _____

_____

_____

_____

2 Label the pictures.

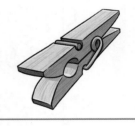

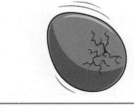

3 Circle the rhyming words in each row.

cog   leg   sag   peg   beg

net   sat   met   but   vet

1 ✏️ Label each pet.

cat	bird	dog	frog

fish	mouse	horse	rabbit

 _____

 _____

 _____

 _____

 _____

 _____

 _____

 _____

2 Join each pet to its home.

1 Color the end sound.

(d) (t) (g)

(d) (t) (g)

(d) (t) (g)

(d) (t) (g)

(d) (t) (g)

(d) (t) (g)

2 Circle the word that matches the picture.

| pet | leg | wet | peg | jet |

| bet | egg | met | net | sat |

| get | wet | vet | put | hot |

3

e = ●
g = ✿
l = ■
b = ▲
p = ★

Crack the code!

■ ● ✿ _____

▲ ● ✿ _____

● ✿ ✿ _____

Reading eggs First Grade Workbook

1 Finish the sentences.

cat   dog   frog   rabbit

My pet is a

_____ .

My pet is a

_____ .

My pet is a

_____ .

My pet is a

_____ .

I finished this lesson online. 	**This egg hatched.**	**I can** read and write: eg and et words.	**I can read** 

1 ✏️ Make a rainbow word. 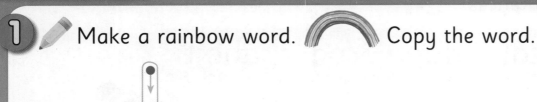 Copy the word.

where ------------------------------------

2 Match each sentence to a picture.

Where you can sleep.

Where you can play.

Where you can eat.

Where you can climb.

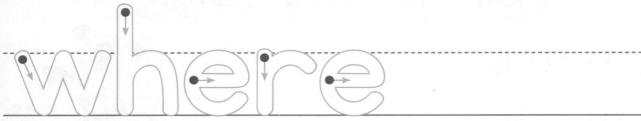

3 Finish the sentences using **Where** or **When**.

_____ are you?

_____ are you going?

_____ is the cat?

_____ will we be there?

where
un

1 Put the letters through the machine. What words can you make?

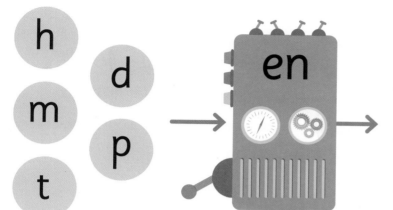

h

d

m

p

t

en

_____

_____

_____

_____

_____

2 Color the **eg** words yellow, **en** words **red** and **et** words **green**.

ten	beg	men	wet
peg	Meg	get	pen
vet	leg	pet	hen

3 Sort the words into their word families.

eg	**en**	**et**
_____	_____	_____
_____	_____	_____
_____	_____	_____
_____	_____	_____

where
un

1 Circle the ladder. Color the slide.

2 Color the correct word. ✗ Cross out the wrong word.

You go [up] [down] the ladder.

You go [up] [down] the slide.

3 Add **ing** to these doing words.

climb_____   walk_____

look_____   talk_____

4 Put the words above into these sentences.

Sam is _____ the ladder.

Jazz is _____ away.

Sid is _____ at the slide.

Meg is _____ to Sam.

Reading eggs First Grade Workbook

Read, then answer the questions.

Sliding

Where is Meg the hen going?
She is climbing up the ladder. Up! Up!
When is Meg coming down?
Wheeeee! Meg is sliding down.
Sliding is a lot of fun.

1 This story is about _____ .
a running   **b** sliding   **c** walking

2 Complete. Meg is _____ the ladder.
a sliding   **b** talking   **c** climbing

3 Order the sentences. Number 1 to 3.
☐ Sit down at the top.
☐ Slide down.
☐ Climb up.

4 Do you like sliding too? _____

I finished this lesson online.	This egg hatched.		I can read and write: the word where, and un words	I can read

en eg

1 Say the word. Join the letters. ✏️ Write.

b	p	o	g
e	g	n	t

p̶e̶g̶

m	a	t	c
n	g	e	n

_____

h	i	t	m
e	n	o	a

_____

i	n	l	e
e	r	o	g

_____

2 ✏️ Write the end sound.

me____   be____   le____   ve____

3 ✏️ Write the words.

n_____   r_____   M_____

1 Read each sentence. Match to a picture.

Five hens. Ten legs.

Ned gets a red egg on legs.

The eggs on legs get fed.
Peck. Peck. Peck.

The eggs on legs get wet
and get into bed.

2 Put the words in the correct order. ✏ Write each sentence.

see Can eggs you legs? on

_____

_____

egg in jet. A legs a on green

_____

_____

1 Use the wheels to make words. 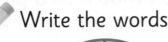 Write the words.

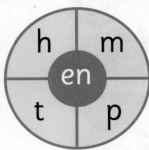

h | m
en
t | p

_____

_____

_____

_____

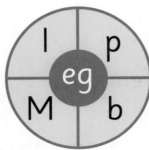

l | p
eg
M | b

_____

_____

_____

_____

2 Circle the words that rhyme.

vet	cat	met	beg	get	pet
bed	jet	red	fed	ten	led
leg	Meg	bet	peg	set	beg
hen	men	Ben	keg	when	ten

3 Write a sentence about the picture.

_____

_____

Read and answer the questions.

Story 1
Eggs on legs can ride in jets. They see red hens who peck, peck, peck.

Story 2
The red egg on legs has got ten pets. They beg to be fed. She puts them to bed.

1 Which story has a red egg on legs?
a Story 1   **b** Story 2

2 How many pets has the red egg on legs?
a one   **b** ten   **c** five

3 Which story has an egg on legs in jets?
a Story 1   **b** Story 2

4 What can the egg on legs in jets see?
a pets   **b** eggs   **c** hens

5 What are story 1 and story 2 about?
a jets   **b** pets   **c** eggs on legs

I finished this lesson online.	This egg hatched.	I can read and write: en and eg words.	I can read

1 Trace and write the words.

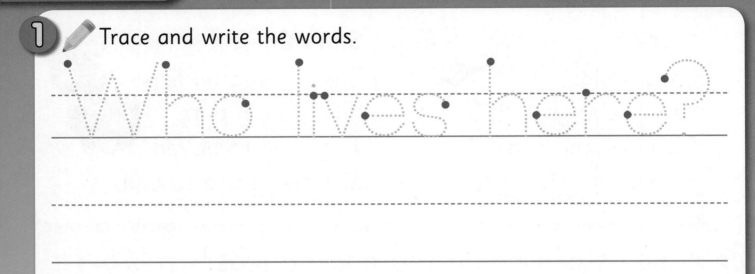

Who lives here?

2 Write the word in a box.

here   who   lives

3 Use the words to complete the sentences.

_____ lives in a nest?

A bird _____ in a nest.

Birds live _____ .

who lives

1 Who lives here? Match the animal picture to its name and then to its home.

bird

dolphin

monkey

butterfly

turtle

fish

elephant

tiger

jungle

sea

tree

2 Put the words in the correct order. Write the sentence.

can up tree. Birds into a fly

_____

_____

1 ✏️ Who lives here?

A _____ lives here.

cat   bird   fish

A _____ lives here.

cat   bird   fish

A _____ lives here.

duck   dog   dolphin

A _____ lives here.

duck   dog   dolphin

2 What can the animals do?

run   climb

The monkey can _____.

The zebra can _____.

Read, then answer the questions.

Who lives here?

Who lives in the sea?
You can find dolphins here.
They like to swim and play in the sea.
Can you see the tree?
Birds live here in nests.
Here is a monkey.
He likes to climb in the jungle.

1 Yes or no?

Dolphins can live in trees.	**a** yes	**b** no
Birds live in nests.	**a** yes	**b** no
Monkeys climb in the sea.	**a** yes	**b** no

2 Which animals like to swim in the sea?
a monkeys   **b** dolphins   **c** birds

3 Which animal likes to climb in the jungle?
a monkey   **b** dolphin   **c** bird

4 Where do you live? _____

I finished this lesson online.	This egg hatched.	I can read and write the words: who, lives, and here.	I can read

1 ✏️ Make a rainbow word. 🌈 Copy the word.

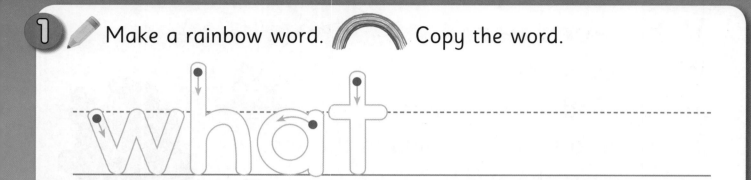

what

_____

2 Color **when** = **red**, color **what** = **green**.

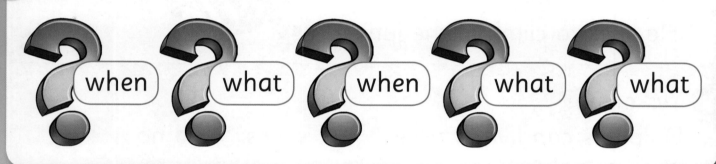

when what when what what

3 Finish each sentence with a word from the box.

What Who When Where

_____ is that girl?

_____ is the band playing?

_____ is the party?

_____ is in the lake?

what

1 🖊 Join each word to a picture.

tail

eye

fire

wing

dragon

claws

---

2 (Circle) the correct word. ✗ Cross out the wrong word.

The dog has a little wing tail .

My cat has big claws fire .

That fire eye is very hot.

This boy dragon has wings and claws.

---

3 Find the animal words and color them. dolphin = **blue**,
dragon = **red**, butterfly = **purple**, monkey = **orange**

d	o	l	p	h	i	n	m	o	n	k	e	y
b	u	t	t	e	r	f	l	y	h	y	m	e
a	r	e	d	r	a	g	o	n	u	t	h	s

1 Complete the sentence for each picture. Use these words.

> yellow orange fire spikes tail

 I can see a red _____.

 I can see _____.

 I can see _____.

2 What is in the lake? Draw your own picture.

3 Write the answer.

What is in the lake?

_____

_____

_____

Reading eggs First Grade Workbook

what

Read, then answer the questions.

What is in the tree?
Sam is in the forest.
He looks up at a tree.
He sees a red wing,
Then he sees a green tail
and a black eye.
Sam climbs the tree and
sees a bird in a nest.

1) Who is in the forest?
a Jazz   **b** a dragon   **c** Sam

2) What color is the wing?
a black   **b** red   **c** green

3) The tail is _____ ?
a green   **b** black   **c** red

4) Why does Sam climb the tree?
a he is sad   **b** he wants to see   **c** he is hot

5) What is in the tree?
a a forest   **b** a bird   **c** a dragon

I finished this lesson online.	This egg hatched.	I can read and write the word: what.	I can read
		☺	

1 Find and (circle) these words. **where what when who**

w	h	o	h	e	w
t	a	w	h	a	t
o	w	h	e	n	o
w	h	e	r	e	w

2 Write the word in a box.

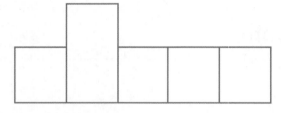
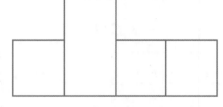
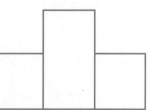
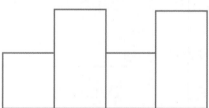

3 Read each sentence. Is it telling us **who**, **what**, **when**, or **where**? Label it.

There is a party. _____

The party is at 8. _____

The king is coming. _____

It is at the castle. _____

ell

1 Put the letters through the word machine.
Write the words you make.

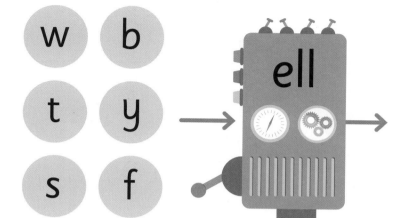

_____

_____

_____

_____

_____

_____

2 Finish the **ell** words.

___ell

___ell

___ell

___ell

___ ___ell

___ ___ell

3 Color **ell** words yellow.

ball   pull   bell   tell   mill   well   sell   full

1 Say the name of each picture. Color its beginning sound, then its ending. Write the word.

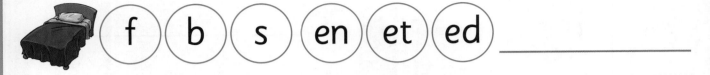

(f) (b) (s) (en) (et) (ed) _____

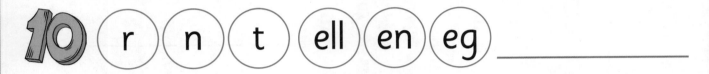

(r) (n) (t) (ell) (en) (eg) _____

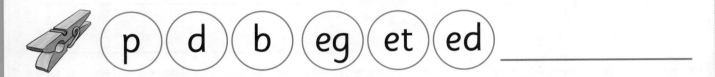

(p) (d) (b) (eg) (et) (ed) _____

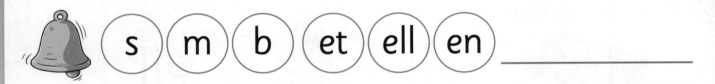

(s) (m) (b) (et) (ell) (en) _____

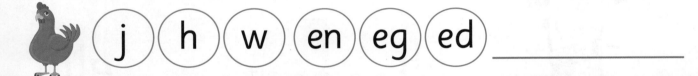

(j) (h) (w) (en) (eg) (ed) _____

2 Finish the words. Use these sounds. **ell ed et eg**

Zen Ten has a cat.

The cat has a bad l_____ .

He has to stay in b_____ .

Zen Ten gets the v_____ .

The cat will soon be w_____ .

ell

1 Make words with these letters.

2-letter word:

3-letter word:

4-letter word:

2 Complete the crossword.
Use the pictures clues to help you.

1.
2.
3.
4.
5.
6.
7.

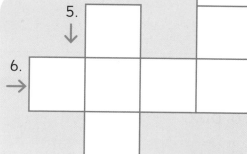

1. ↓
3. ↓
2. →
5. ↓
4. →
6. →
7. →

Review

1 Color · ell ◄ et ◄ en ◄ ed ◄ eg ◄

2 ✏️ Sort the words into their word families.

eg	ed	ell	en	et

3 ✏️ Write the word in a box.

beg   red   shell   pen   let

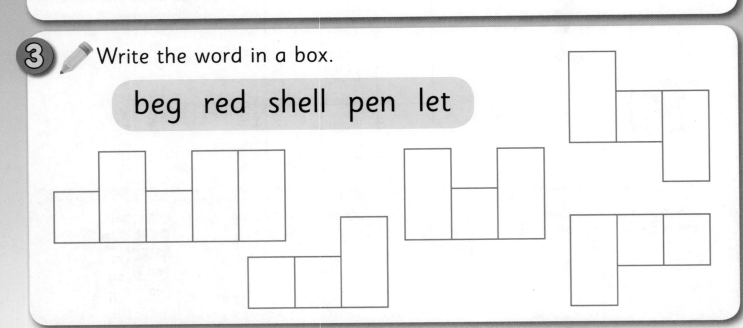

82   Reading eggs First Grade Workbook

Review

1 Match each picture to a word.

| plate | cup | bag | hat |

2 Match each word to a number.

| 1 | 2 | 3 | 4 | 5 | 6 | 7 |

seven   one

three   six   four

five   two

3 Color the party words **red** and the number words **blue**.

| one | party | five | hat | six |

| bag | birthday | ten | two | band |

4 Color the correct word. ✗ Cross out the wrong word.

Today is my (balloon birthday).

I am (see six) years old.

Please come to my (party plate).

1 Complete the sentences. Use every word once.

> party birthday cups plate and
> seven Meg Sam bags hat hats

_____ is having a _____

_____ .

Meg has _____ plates, seven

_____ , seven _____ , and

seven _____ .

_____ gets a _____ , a cup,

a _____ , _____ a bag.

2 Read and draw.

seven green hats   three green plates

1. ✏ Number the events in the correct order from 1—4.

2. Match each sentence to its picture.

Making a birthday cake

Put it in the oven. ☐

Put everything into a bowl. ☐

Here is the birthday cake! ☐

Mix it all up well. ☐

3. ✏ When is **your** birthday?

_____

1 Say the name of each picture. Color the word family.

(ed) (et)   (eg) (uck)   (ell) (en)   (uck) (ell)

2 Circle the rhyming words in each row.

pen	pet	ten	men	beg
leg	get	peg	Meg	well
bet	set	bed	Ben	pet
tell	fed	bell	shell	den
red	bed	duck	fed	peg

3 Make words with these letters.

e   w   e   h   r

2-letter word: ◯ ◯

4-letter word: ◯ ◯ ◯

5-letter word: ◯ ◯ ◯ ◯ ◯

Reading eggs First Grade Workbook

MAP 8 LESSONS 71 TO 80

Quiz

4 Color the answer.

Who lives in the sea?

(elephant)   (cat)

(tiger)   (dolphin)

Who lives in the jungle?

(monkey)   (dog)

(fish)   (rabbit)

5 Complete each sentence.

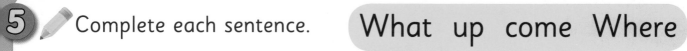 What   up   come   Where

_____ is Sam going?

I am climbing _____ the ladder.

Here _____ my dogs.

_____ is in the tree?

6 Look at the picture. ✓Check the matching sentence.
✗Cross the wrong sentence.

☐ Meg the hen gets ten red pens.

☐ Meg the hen gets ten blue pens.

7 Draw.

six yellow pets

ten red eggs

Well Done!

YOU COMPLETED

MAP 8

YOU CAN:

☐ Recognize the: **ed, eg, et, en,** and **ell** word families.

☐ Read and write the words: **my, come, play, lives, where, who, when,** and **what**.

☐ Read other words such as: **cracking, rolling, climbing, sliding, wing, tail, spike, monkey, dolphin,** and **dragon**.

☐ Read lots of sentences:
This is my pet. My pet is a rabbit.

☐ Read these books:

Follow the instructions to set the table for the party.

1 Color the plates **yellow**.

2 Draw seven **red** cups.

3 Color the cake in **blue** and **purple**.

4 Draw seven **green** hats.

5 Put seven **pink** candles on the cake.

Happy Birthday Meg

Meg is 7 today

1 Make words. ✏ Write them.

h t d s i p _____
_____
_____
_____

2 Use the letters to make words.

h f j _____ og
_____ og
_____ og

m y s _____ uck
_____ uck
_____ uck

3 Say the name of each picture. Color its beginning sound, then its ending. ✏ Write the word.

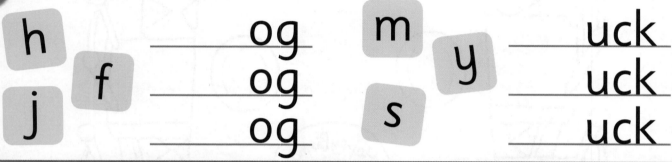

10 (p)(t)(m)(og)(ip)(en) _____

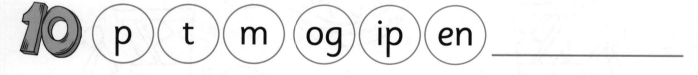

(b)(s)(z)(uck)(ip)(og) _____

(l)(r)(d)(og)(en)(ip) _____

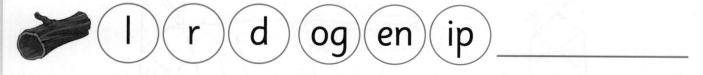

(m)(t)(d)(ip)(uck)(en) _____

Reading eggs First Grade Workbook

1 Make a rainbow word. Copy the word.

with

2 Find the words. Color **with red**, **what blue** and **have green**.

w	i	t	h	w	h	a	t	h	a	v	e
h	a	v	e	w	i	t	h	w	h	a	t
w	h	a	t	h	a	v	e	w	i	t	h

3 Complete each sentence. Use the words **with**, **what**, and **have**.

I _____ blue eyes.

I can see _____ my eyes.

_____ do you smell with?

You smell _____ your nose.

4 Write the word in a box.

what   with   when

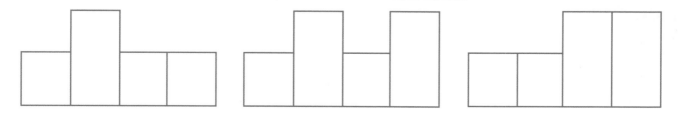

1 Join each word to a picture.

eyes

ears

nose

mouth

hands

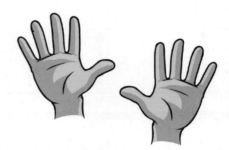

2 ✏️ Label the picture. hear see touch taste smell

s _____

h _____

t _____

s _____

t _____

3 Put the words in the correct order to make a sentence.

can ears. I my with hear

_____

_____

with

 Write three things that you can:

see

_____

_____

touch

_____

_____

_____

smell

_____

_____

_____

hear

_____

_____

_____

taste

_____

_____

_____

I finished this lesson online. 	This egg hatched.	I can read and write the word with, and read and write about the five senses.	I can read

1 Color the word **pie**.

pie	pie	pet
pin	pie	pie

2 Circle the **ie** words.

pin   pie   six   lit   lie

pit   fig   tie   bit   die

3 Make plurals by adding **s**. Write each word.

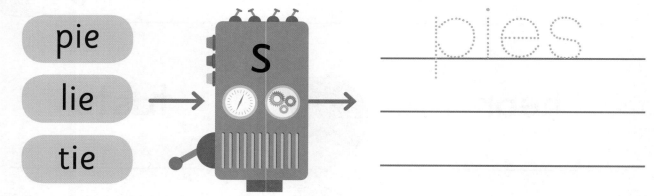

pie → **s** → pies

lie → _____

tie → _____

4 Get Smile the crocodile to his pie. Follow the trail of **ie** words.

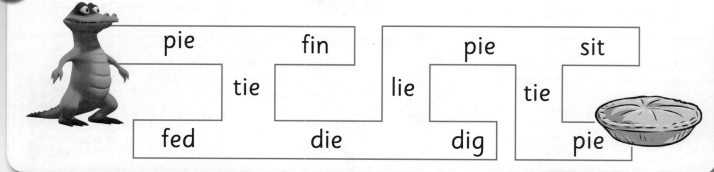

pie   fin   pie   sit

tie   lie   tie

fed   die   dig   pie

Reading eggs First Grade Workbook

1 Color each picture that has an **ie** sound.

2 Draw lines to match.

cries   pie   fries   ties

3 Circle the correct words.

pie
tie
lie

fries
cries
ties

cries
tie
pie

4 How many sounds in each word?

p i e   p i e s   t i e   t i e s
• —   • — •   • —   • — •

| 1 | 2 | 3 | | 1 | 2 | 3 | | 1 | 2 | 3 | | 1 | 2 | 3 |

1 Match the words to their pictures.

picnic   shop   crocodile   apple   pie   smile

2 Label the pies.

peach
apple
big
little

 _____ pie

 _____ pie

 _____ pie

_____ pie

3 Put the words in order to make a sentence.

is   a   pie.   little   Here

_____

_____

Read, then answer the questions.

Smile's pie

Smile the crocodile is going to a picnic.
He wants to take an apple pie.
Smile runs to the pie shop.
He sees a little pie, a big pie, a peach pie, and a plum pie.
Then Smile sees an apple pie. Hooray!

1 Smile is going to _____.

a a party   **b** a picnic   **c** bed

2 He wants to take _____.

a a big pie   **b** a plum pie   **c** an apple pie

3 Smile runs to the _____.

a pie shop   **b** picnic   **c** park

4 Write 2 pies Smile sees.

_____ and _____

5 Does Smile find an apple pie?

a yes   **b** no

I finished this lesson online.	This egg hatched.	I can read and write: ie words.	I can read

1 Join each letter to the **ine** machine. ✏ Write the three words.

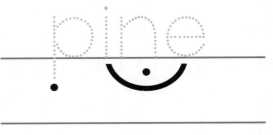

pine

2 Color the **ine** words **yellow**, **ike** words **red**.

like	mine	pine	bike
hike	pike	line	nine

3 Sort the words above into their word families ✏ Write.

ine

ike

_____

_____

_____

_____

_____

_____

_____

_____

4 Complete the **long i** words.

 p_____

 b_k_

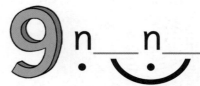 n_n_

1 Match up the pairs.

sister

father

aunt

grandfather

mother

brother

grandmother

uncle

2 Color the correct word.

My [mop] [mom] had a baby boy.

He is my [brother] [sister] .

Our [plants] [parents] take care of us.

We are a [farm] [family] .

3 Match each word to a picture.

walk   **shoe lace**   **read**   **ride**

i–e

1 Match the sentences to their pictures.

I help my brother tie his shoe laces.

My father helps me ride my bike.

My family gave me a party.

Our mother helps us write a story.

2 Write a sentence using the words **help** and **sister**. Draw a picture.

Reading **eggs** First Grade Workbook

i–e

Read, then answer the questions.

Family bike ride

On Sundays, my family goes for a bike ride.
We like to ride in the park.
We all set off at nine and ride in one long line.
I like to ride my bike with my family.
It makes me smile.

1 When are the family bike rides?
  a Monday   **b** Sunday   **c** Saturday

2 Where do they ride?
  a to school   **b** to the party   **c** to the park

3 What time do they set off?
  a nine   **b** five   **c** ten

4 They all ride in one long _____.
  a time   **b** mine   **c** line

5 What do **you** do on Sundays?

_____

I finished this lesson online.	This egg hatched.		I can read and write: i–e words, and family words.	I can read

ine

1 Use the wheels to make words. Write the words.

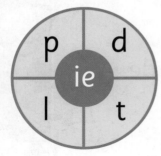
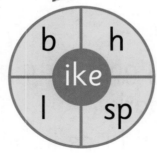
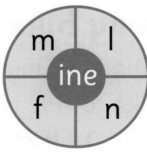

_____   _____   _____

_____   _____   _____

_____   _____   _____

_____   _____   _____

2 Color the **ine** words.

mine	bike	vine
pie	nine	ties
pine	line	fine
	ride	

3 Circle the rhyming words in each row.

| vine | hike | dine | pies | fine |

| hike | line | bike | tie | like |

| line | nine | fries | mine | spike |

1 Say the word. Join the letters. ✏️ Write.

| d | p | s | a |
| n | o | i → e | |

p _____

| n | i | h | m |
| a | e | n | e |

_____

| d | b | m | u |
| a | i | t | e |

_____

| p | t | i | a |
| o | f | n | e |

_____

2 ✏️ Write the end sound.   ine   ike   ile

sm_____

v_____

b_____

n_____

3 ✏️ Complete Spine the Porcupine's word chain.
Use a different letter each time.

| dine | __ine | __ine | __ine | __ine |

ine

1 Match each picture to a word.

track

crash

fell

bike

wobble

ride

2 Color the correct word. ✗ Cross out the wrong word.

Charlie wants to 「ride / crash」 his bike.

The bike 「wobbled / fell」 a bit.

Charlie 「fall / fell」 off the bike.

The bike went 「crash / truck」 .

Charlie does not want to 「fall / fell」 off.

Reading eggs First Grade Workbook

ine

1 (Circle) the sentence that matches the pictures.

Jazz the cat can run very fast.

Jazz the cat can ride a bike.

Charlie likes this red bike.

Charlie gives his bike to Jazz.

Charlie rides down the track.

Charlie wobbles and falls off.

"I can ride my bike!" says Charlie.

"I do not like this bike," says Charlie.

2 Put the words in the correct order. ✏️ Write each sentence.

can   red   Charlie   bike.   his   ride

_____

back   his   got   bike.   on   Charlie

_____

| I finished this lesson online.  | This egg hatched. | I can read and write: ine words, and i–e words. | I can read |

sh

1 Join Shelly Shark to the shells. ✏️ Write each word.

sh

ip

op

ow

_____

_____

_____

2 Color the **sh** words.

| shell | sheep | sock | shop | shirt |

| shark | slug | swan | shed | sun |

3 Say the name of each picture. Color its beginning sound, middle, then its ending sound. ✏️ Write the word.

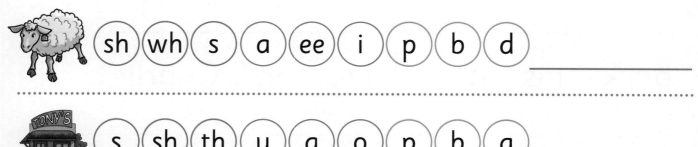

sh wh s a ee i p b d _____

s sh th u a o p b q _____

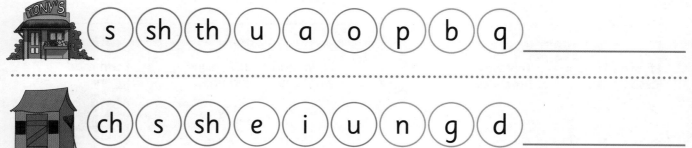

ch s sh e i u n g d _____

1 Join each word to a picture.

shell

shop

sheep

shed

shark

shoes

2 Complete each sentence and ✏ draw a picture.

shell   sheep   shirt

A shark in a _____ .

A _____ in a shop.

A _____ on a shed.

1 Color the correct word. ✗ Cross out the wrong word.

I love to eat hot (shoes) (chips) .

Shelley buys food at the (shops) (sheep) .

2 Read each sentence and match to a picture.

I can see a shark in a shirt.

There is a big sheep on my shed.

Come to the shop that sells shells.

3 Put the words in the correct order. ✏ Write the sentence.

Shark   going   shops.   Shelley   the   loves   to

_____

4 ✏ Write a sentence. Use the words   shark   shoes   shop

_____

_____

Read, then answer the questions.

Shelley's shirt

Shelley is going shopping.
She wants a new shirt for Jazz's party.
This shop sells shiny shoes.
That shop sells big, white shells.
Shelley sees a shirt shop.
She buys a blue shirt with shells on it.

1 Why does Shelley go shopping?
   a to get a shell   **b** to get shoes   **c** to get a shirt

2 Who is having a party?
   a Shelley   **b** Jazz   **c** Sam

3 One shop sells _____ shoes.
   a shiny   **b** big   **c** white

4 One shop sells white _____.
   a shoes   **b** shirts   **c** shells

5 Write 2 things about the shirt.
   1. _____   2. _____

1 Join the puzzle pieces. Write the words.

sh e l f _____

sh o r t s _____

sh o e s _____

2 Use the letters to make words.

sh

ip _____ _____ ine

_____ eet _____ op

irt _____ _____ ovel

3 Write the word in a box.

shore

shut

shell

shiny

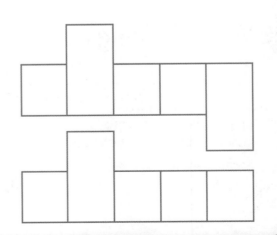

sh

1 Join each word to a picture.

shovel

shelf

shorts

ship

shirt

shoelaces

2 Write the words in the correct box.

shell shoes shark shirt ships shorts

sea	**clothes**
_____	_____
_____	_____
_____	_____

3 Use the words above to complete the sentences.

A _____ has big, sharp teeth.

I wear _____ on my feet.

1 ✏️ Put the words in order to make a sentence.

This   short.   shirt   too   is

_____

shop.   Let's   into   this   go

_____

2 ✏️ Complete the sentences.   shirt shiny shop shoes

Shelley shark is going to the

_____ .

Shelley wants to buy a new

_____ .

Shoe sheep wants to buy new

_____ .

These shoes are very

_____ .

sh

Read, then answer the questions.

My shed

I have a shed in the garden.
There are old shoes and
lots of shells in the shed.
I have a shelf where I keep my
toy ship. It has a shiny bell.
My shed is where my bike lives.

1 Where is my shed?

  a in the park   **b** in the garden   **c** on a shelf

2 The ships bell is _____ .

  a big   **b** old   **c** shiny

3 Write 4 things I keep in my shed.

  1. _____   2. _____

  3. _____   4. _____

4 What else can you keep in a shed?

_____

5 Circle all the **sh** words in the story.

I finished this lesson online.	This egg hatched.	I can read and write: lots of sh words.	I can read

1 Use the wheels to make words. Write the words.

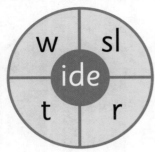
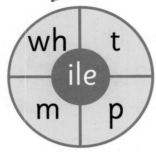
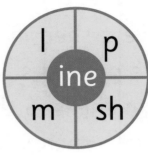

_____   _____   _____

_____   _____   _____

_____   _____   _____

_____   _____   _____

2 Color **ire** words **pink**, **ipe** words **red**, **ite** words **blue**, **ive** words **green**.

| site | dive | wire | fire |

| pipe | bite | wipe | hire |

| kite | hive | five | ripe |

3 Sort the words above into their word families. Write.

ire	ipe	ite	ive

1 Say the name of each picture. Color its beginning sound, then its ending. Write the word.

(l) (k) (s) (ide) (ire) (ite) _____

(h) (n) (m) (ive) (ile) (ine) _____

(r) (p) (f) (ite) (ire) (ide) _____

(p) (d) (b) (ine) (ile) (ipe) _____

(v) (f) (h) (ire) (ive) (ide) _____

2 Finish the sentences. Use these word endings.

ike
ive
ite
ipe

Sid wants to fly his k_____ today.

This banana is very r_____ .

Sam can ride his big red b_____ .

These bees live in a h_____ .

3 Circle the hidden **i–e** words.

milepinefirewipebite

How many words did you circle? _____

1 Join each word to a picture.

ride

tie

spine

smile

nine

kite

2 Match the opposites.

 big

 sad

 short

 happy

 tall

 little

3 Use the opposites to complete the sentences.

black   cold   hot   white

The zebra has _____ and _____ stripes.

Ice is _____ and fire is _____ .

1 Complete the sentences.

slide Smile ride bite

Let's go for a _____ in Jet set.

Have a _____ of my apple.

Say hello to _____ the crocodile.

Climb up the ladder and _____ down.

2 Crack the code!

i = ✿
m = ★
l = ✚
e = ▲
n = ♥

★ ✿ ♥ ▲

_____

✚ ✿ ★ ▲

_____

★ ✿ ✚ ▲

_____

✚ ✿ ♥ ▲

_____

3 Write a sentence with one word from above.

_____

_____

I finished this lesson online.	This egg hatched.	I can read and write i–e words, and I know some opposite words.	I can read
		☺	

1 Join Charlie Chimp to the bananas. Write the words.

ch

op    in

at    eek

_____

_____

_____

_____

2 Color **ch** words **red**, **sh** words **yellow**.

shop	cheep	chips	shed
sheep	shoes	chain	chew
cheeky	chest	shed	cheese

3 Join the puzzle pieces. Write the word. Join to a picture.

ips

ch

ick

eese

op

ch _____

_____

_____

_____

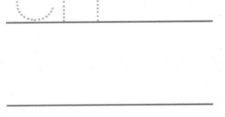

1 Match the words to a picture.

chick

chain

chips

chimp

cheese

child

2 Finish the sentences.

chomp   cheese   chat   chin

 I can see some _____ .

 The moon has a big _____ .

 The horse likes to _____ .

 They like to _____ .

1 Color the correct word. ✗ Cross out the wrong word.

We buy shoes at the (chop) (shop) .

Cheese is good to (chew) (shoe) .

"Cheep, cheep!" says the little (chin) (chick).

Charlie is a cheeky (chimp) (chomp).

We can (chest) (chase) the chicks at the farm.

2 ✏ Write a sentence using each word.

chin _____

_____

chat _____

_____

chomp _____

_____

ch

Read, then answer the questions.

Cheeky chick, cheeky chimp

I am a cheeky chick.
I like to eat cheese, chips, and chops.
Chomp, chomp, chomp!
He is a cheeky chimp.
He likes to chat all day to lots of chimps.
Chat! Chat! Chat!

1 This chick is _____ .
   a chatty   **b** cheeky   **c** chewy

2 The chick likes to eat:

   1. _____ 2. _____ 3. _____

3 The chimp has:
   a a big chest   **b** a bag of chips   **c** cheese

4 Who does the chimp like to chat to?
   a a chick   **b** a child   **c** chimps

5 Who do **you** like to chat to?

   _____

I finished this lesson online.	This egg hatched.	I can read and write: lots of ch words.	I can read

1 Color the **th** words.

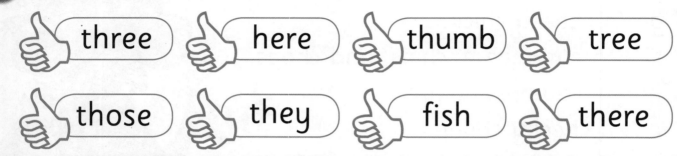

three   here   thumb   tree

those   they   fish   there

2 Use the letters to make the words.

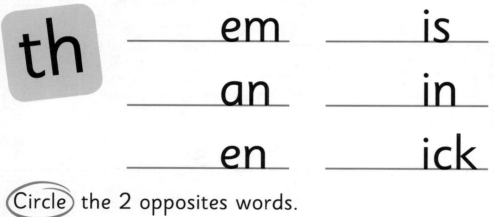

th

_____ em   _____ is

_____ an   _____ in

_____ en   _____ ick

(Circle) the 2 opposites words.

3 How many sounds in each word?

t h i s
— · ·
| 2 | 3 | 4 |

t h i n k
— · · ·
| 2 | 3 | 4 |

t h a t
— · ·
| 2 | 3 | 4 |

t h u d s
— · · ·
| 2 | 3 | 4 |

th

1 Match the words to a picture.

thorn

thumb

thin

thick

2 Fill the cupboard. Write the things you can eat on the shelves.

fridge

apple

cheese

hats

chicken

chips

socks

cherries

books

sandwich

peach

home

chocolate

roast beef

1 Color the correct word.

Then / That is a good shop.

Then / There is that cheeky chimp.

2 Match the sentences to their pictures.

This little critter went to the shop.

She got a box of cherries.

He got a block of chocolate.

3 Choose the correct word for each sentence.

stayed   none   empty

This critter _____ home .

This fridge was _____ .

This little critter had _____ .

1 Read, then number the sentences in the correct order from 1–5. Match to a picture.

☐ He got chicken and chips, and a block of chocolate.

☐ Now there is lots of food in the fridge and the cupboard.

☐ The critters go to the shop. These critters stay at home.

☐ There is no food. The fridge is empty. The cupboard is empty.

☐ They had fun at the shop. Now its time to go home.

2 What to do you like to eat?

_____

I finished this lesson online.	This egg hatched.		I can read and write: th words.	I can read
89			😊	This little critter

1 Use the wheels to make words. Write the words.

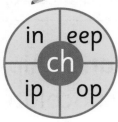
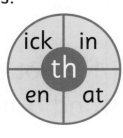

_____   _____   _____

_____   _____   _____

_____   _____   _____

_____   _____   _____

2 Color **ide** yellow, **ile** pink, **ine** blue, **ive** orange.

(mile) (five) (hide) (nine) (hive) (pine)

(side) (tile) (dive) (smile) (ride) (fine)

3 Sort the words above into their word families. Write.

ide	ile	ine	ive

4 Write the word in a box.

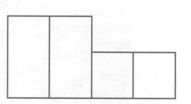
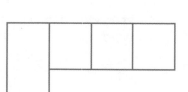
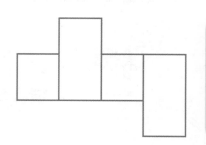

pies

chop

thin

Reading eggs First Grade Workbook

1 🖊 Write three words for each family.

sh_____   ch_____   th_____

sh_____   ch_____   th_____

sh_____   ch_____   th_____

2 🖊 Write a word that **ends** in:

_____sh   _____ch   _____th

3 Change one letter at a time. Complete the word ladder.

bi____e

____ike

hi____e

____ive

h   r   v

fi____e

fi____e

t   k   b

4 🖊 Write a sentence using the word **shoes**.

_____

_____

1 Trace and copy.

together

mixed

2 Use the correct word from above to finish the sentences.

Charlie put the cherries and the chocolate

_____ .

He _____ them up.

3 Put the foods in the mixer with the chips. Write the new foods.

choc

cheese

egg

chicken

banana

choc chips

_____

_____

_____

1 ✏️ Finish the sentences.

| cherries | chocolate | chicken | chips |

 Charlie likes chewing on _____ .

 Charlie likes chomping on _____ .

 Charlie likes chewing on _____ .

 Charlie likes chomping on _____ .

2 ✏️ Write the last sentence.

 _____

_____

3 ✏️ Complete the sentences.

Shelley Shark likes shopping for _____ .

Smile the Crocodile likes _____ .

| I finished this lesson online.  | This egg hatched. | I can read and write: i–e, sh, ch, and th words. | I can read |

1 Say the name of each picture. Color the word family.

 ive · ime

 ike · ile

 ide · ire

 ite · ine

2 Circle the rhyming words in each row.

mine	pies	slide	ties	lies
bike	file	hike	time	like
ride	wipe	ripe	dine	pipe

3 Make words with these letters.   h   w   t   i

2-letter word: ◯ ◯

3-letter word: ◯ ◯ ◯

4-letter word: ◯ ◯ ◯ ◯

4 ✏ Write the word in a box.

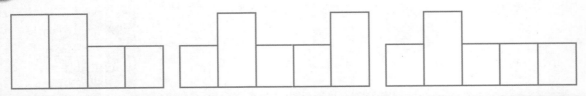

chick

shoes

thin

Reading eggs First Grade Workbook

MAP 9 LESSONS 81 TO 90 **Quiz**

5 Color the correct word.

(This) (These) shoes have shoelaces.

Shelley wants to (new) (buy) a (new) (buy) shirt.

(This) (These) shirt has too many ships.

6 Complete the sentences.

nose   eyes   ears

I can see with my _____.

I can hear with my _____.

I can smell with my _____.

7 Look at the picture. ✓Check the matching sentence.
✗Cross the wrong sentence.

☐ This cheeky chimp likes cherries.

☐ This cheeky chimp goes shopping.

☐ Cheeky chimps likes chips and cheese.

8 Draw. Cheeky Charlie likes

cherry chocolate.

chicken chips.

Nice Work!

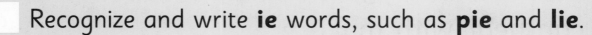

YOU COMPLETED

MAP 9

YOU CAN:

- [ ] Recognize and write **ie** words, such as **pie** and **lie**.
- [ ] Recognize and write **i–e** words, such as **ine, ike, ile, ide, ite,** and **ire**.
- [ ] Read and write the **ch, sh,** and **th** word families.
- [ ] Read and write the word **with**.
- [ ] Read other words such as: **this, these, nose, eyes, ears, mother, father, sister, brother, track, wobble, fridge,** and **cupboard**.
- [ ] Read these books:

Fun Spot 3

1 **Color** **says = red**, **with = green**, where = yellow, **then = pink**,
they = orange, some = blue, **these = purple**, **too = brown**,
this = black

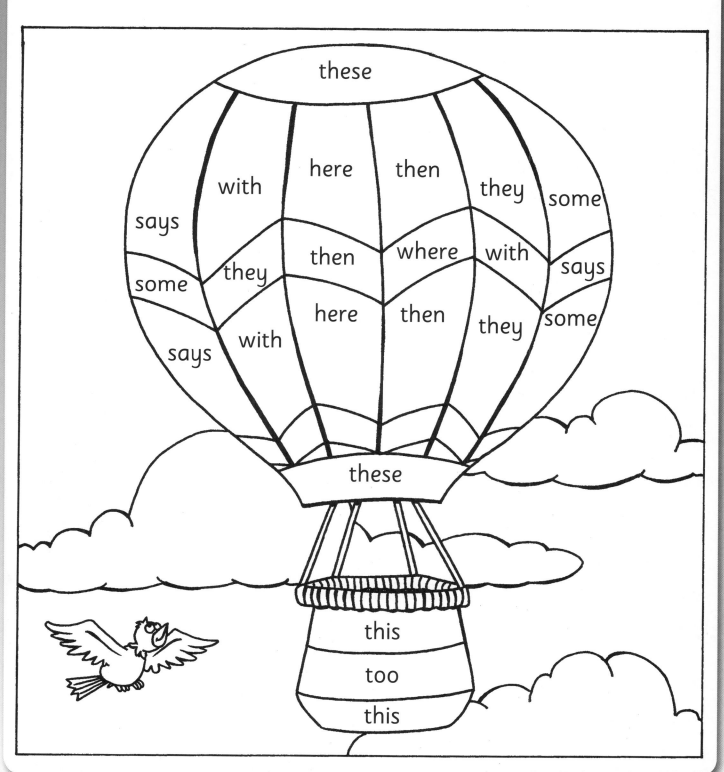

1 Say the word. Color if it starts with **soft c**.

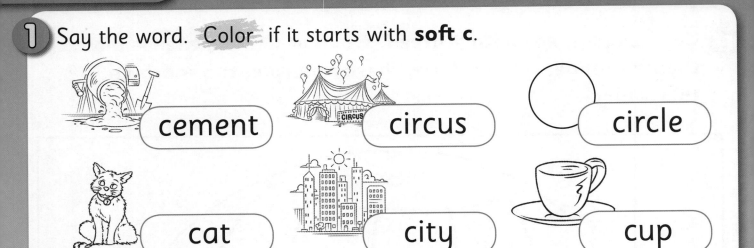

cement   circus   circle

cat   city   cup

2 Make words. Write. Join to a picture.

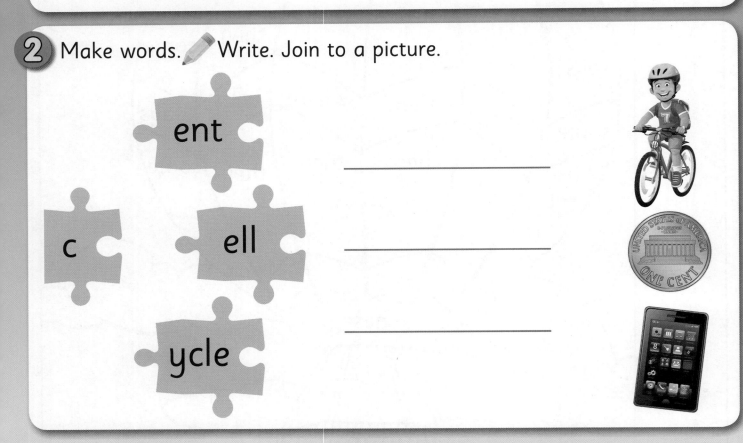

ent

c   ell

ycle

_____

_____

_____

3 Color the **ci** words yellow, **cy** words red, **ce** words green.

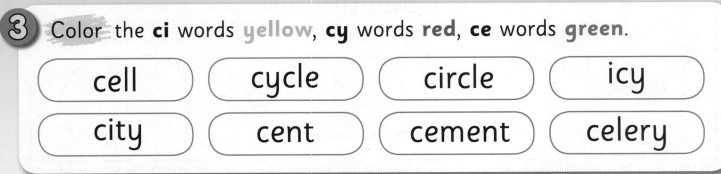

cell   cycle   circle   icy

city   cent   cement   celery

1 Join the kite bike to the word **bicycle**.

bicycle   circle   bicycle

bicycle   bubble

colour   bicycle   bicycle

2 Color the wheels that have a **soft c** sound.

3 Match each picture to a word.

unicycle

bicycle

tricycle

wheel

clown

bike rack

1 Color the correct word. ✗ Cross out the wrong word.

I have two wheels on my (bisycle) (bicycle).

Let's see the funny (circus) (sircus) clowns!

2 (Circle) the **soft c** words.

- Leggy likes to cycle in circles.
- The circus is coming to the city.

Color a circle each time you find a **soft c** word.

◯ ◯ ◯ ◯

Have you been to the circus? _____

3 Choose the correct word for each sentence.

celery   cents   cement

I bought a banana for 50 _____ .

Sam fell off his bike on to the _____ .

She likes to chomp on cheese and _____ .

soft c

Read, then answer the questions.

Cycles

My tricycle has three wheels.
My brother has a bicycle with two wheels.
We ride our cycles together in the park.
Sometime my brother rides to school.
He locks his bike up in the bike rack.

1 How many wheels are on a tricycle?

　a one　　**b** two　　**c** three

2 A bicycle has _____ wheels.

　a three　　**b** two　　**c** one

3 My brother rides a _____ .

　a unicycle　　**b** tricycle　　**c** bicycle

4 Where do we ride our cycles together?

　a park　　**b** school　　**c** circus

5 Why does my brother lock his bike?

　a to fix it　　**b** to keep it safe　　**c** to ride it

I finished this lesson online.	**This egg hatched.**	**I can** read and write words with the soft c sound.	**I can read**

ice

1 Join the **ice** dice to make words. Write. Match to a picture.

m + ice = _____

l + ice = _____

d + ice = _____

r + ice = _____

2 Color the **ice** words **yellow**, **ine** words **red**, **ite** words **green**.

mite	rice	bite	fine	price	vine
nine	mice	site	kite	nice	mine

3 Sort the words into their word families. Write.

ice	ine	ite
_____	_____	_____
_____	_____	_____
_____	_____	_____

ice

1 Put the letters through the word machine.
🖊 Write the words you make.

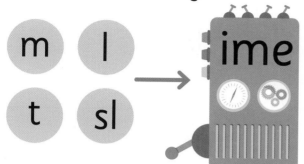

m   l
t   sl   → **ime** → _____
_____
_____
_____

2 Color the **ipe** words.

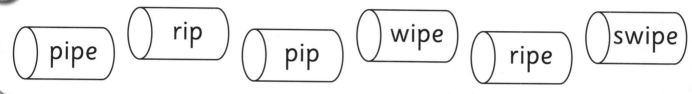

pipe   rip   pip   wipe   ripe   swipe

3 Say the word for the picture. (Circle) the word that rhymes.

wipe   rice   time   kite

wipe   rice   time   kite

4 Use the word wheels to make words. 🖊 Write the words.

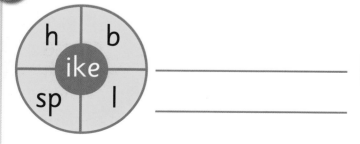

h   b
ike
sp   l

_____
_____
_____

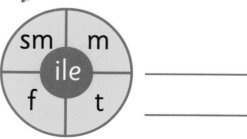

sm   m
ile
f   t

_____
_____
_____

1 Make compound words. Write.

> house box lace ball

 foot + _____ = _____

 sand + _____ = _____

 light + _____ = _____

 shoe + _____ = _____

2 Use the words above to complete the sentences.

She likes to dig in the _____ .

I play _____ in the park with

my brother.

You can see the _____ by the sea.

He helps to tie his sister's _____ .

3 Put the words in order to make a sentence.

ride Five bikes. nice five white mice

_____

_____

ice

1 Complete each sentence.

bites   bedtime   hide

Five white mice _____ in the vine.

Five white mice say no more _____!

And now it's _____!

2 Match the sentences to the pictures.

Five white mice all in a line.

Five white mice fly nine fine kites.

The mites take a hike.
They run and hide.

3 Write a sentence using the words **nice** and **mice**. Draw a picture.

_____

_____

_____

I finished this lesson online.	This egg hatched.		I can read and write: ice words. I can join 2 words together.	I can read
 92				Five white mice

Reading **eggs** First Grade Workbook

141

soft g

1 Say the word. Color if it starts with **soft g**.

gem   gate   gelato   giraffe

grass   gym   gold   giant

2 Join the **soft g** puzzle piece to make words. Write. Join to a picture.

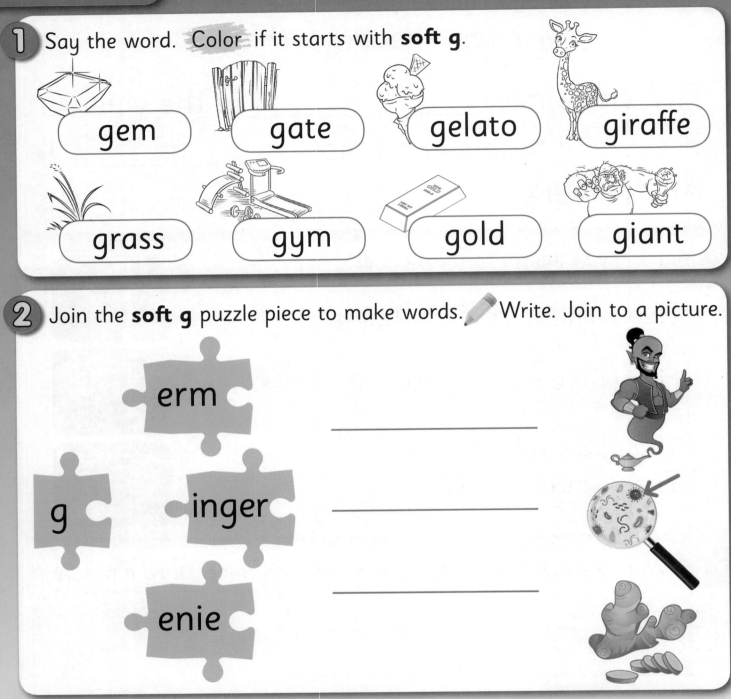

erm

g   inger

enie

_____

_____

_____

3 Color the **gi** words **red**, **gy** words **yellow**, **ge** words **green**.

gym   germ   giant   gelato

giraffe   ginger   genie   gem

Reading eggs First Grade Workbook

soft g

1 Put the letters through the word machine. ✏️ Write the words.

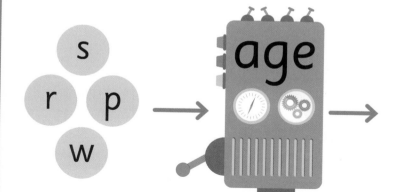

s
r p
w
→ **age** → _____
_____
_____
_____

2 Complete the age words. Match to a picture.

c   r   st   p

_____age   _____age   _____age   _____age

3 Color the **age** words **yellow**.

| page | stage | days | wage | flag |

| rage | sage | bags | cage | age |

1 Trace and write the words.

Saturday --

today --

week --

2 Use the words above to complete the sentences.

There are seven days in a _____.

It is nice and sunny _____.

The birthday party is on _____.

3 Color the correct word.

Today is (sage) (Saturday).

Gemma was going out to eat (giant) (gelato).

She saw two mice in a (cage) (page).

One mouse was little. The other was
a (giraffe) (giant).

soft g

Read, then answer the questions.

Gemma's day

Gemma Giraffe loves Saturdays.
First she goes to the gym. She runs and rides a bike.
Next she goes to the park. She plays and slides.
Then Gemma goes to a show. She wears her
gems and eats a giant gelato. Yum!

1 Which day does Gemma like best?

a Friday   **b** Saturday   **c** Sunday

2 Where does she run?

a park   **b** show   **c** gym

3 Number 1 to 3 in the order they happen.

☐ Gemma gets a gelato.   ☐ Gemma rides a bike.

☐ Gemma plays in the park.

4 What is another word for giant?

a small   **b** yummy   **c** big

5 What is your best day of the week?

_____

I finished this lesson online.	This egg hatched.	I can read and write: silent g words words, and the age word family.	I can read
93		☺	Gemma Giraffe

1 Color the **ake** words.

 cake

 make

 track

 bake

 park

 take

 Jake

 like

2 Use the letters to make words.

w   r   l

_____ ake
_____ ake
_____ ake

d   g   l

_____ ate
_____ ate
_____ ate

3 Label the pictures.

pl _____

l _____

r _____

d _____

J _____

c _____

Reading **eggs** First Grade Workbook

ake

1 Match each word to a picture.

rooster

duck

cake

lake

rake

snake

2 Color the correct word. ✗ Cross out the wrong word.

Jake wants to bake a (rake) (cake).

"Quack!" said Fluff the (snake) (duck).

Let's have a swim in the (lake) (rooster).

I will tidy the leaves with this (rake) (lake).

3 Write the missing words.   **wake   cake   late   plate**

Can I please eat the _____ .

Time to _____ up! You will be _____ .

Put those cakes on that _____ .

ake

1 Read the clue. ✏️ Write the word.

You use me to collect leaves. I am a

r_____ .

You put your food on me. I am a

pl_____ .

You can swim in me. I am a

l_____ .

I taste yummy! I am a

c_____ .

2 Put the words in the correct order. ✏️ Write the sentence.

Jake eat Did the cake? the snake

_____

_____

3 ✏️ Draw a picture for this sentence.

Jake the snake has a cake on a plate.

ake

Read, then answer the questions.

Jake's cake

Sam, Jazz, and Jake the snake are
going for a picnic by the lake.
"I will bake a cake," says Jake.
"A big chocolate cake on a plate."
Jazz will help Jake bake the cake.
Sam will help Jake eat it!

1 Where is the picnic?

a in the park   **b** by the lake   **c** at the shops

2 Who will bake a cake?

a Sam   **b** Jazz   **c** Jake

3 What sort of cake will it be?

a chocolate   **b** ice-cream   **c** banana

4 Who wants to help bake the cake?

a Jake   **b** Sam   **c** Jazz

5 What do you know about Sam?

a He likes singing.   **b** He likes cake.   **c** He likes football.

I finished this lesson online.	This egg hatched.	I can read and write: the ake word family.	I can read

1 Use the wheels to make words. 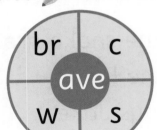 Write the words.

sh | c
ape
gr | t

br | c
ave
w | s

fl | n
ame
s | g

_____   _____   _____

_____   _____   _____

_____   _____   _____

_____   _____   _____

2 Color **ate** words **pink**, **age** words **red**, **ale** words **blue**, **ane** words **green**.

page	male	date	cane
rage	pale	lane	sale
cage	gate	mane	late

3 Sort the words into their word families. Write.

ate	age	ale	ane

1 Say the name of each picture. Color its beginning sound, then its ending. ✏ Write the word.

(j) (g) (d) (age) (ate) (ape) _____

(c) (r) (s) (ate) (ave) (age) _____

(v) (m) (w) (ave) (ale) (age) _____

(t) (l) (h) (ame) (age) (ape) _____

(b) (c) (s) (ale) (ane) (ate) _____

2 Finish the sentences.

| age |
| ave |
| ate |
| ame |

The brown bear sleeps in a c_____.

My n_____ is Sid the Kid.

My two little birds live in a c_____.

What is the d_____ today?

3 Circle the hidden **a–e** words.

milepinefirewipebite

How many words did you circle? _____

1 Match each picture to a word.

 eggs

cake tin

bowl

mix

frosting

pour

2 Complete the crossword. Use the picture clues to help you.

1.

2.

3.

4.

5.

6.

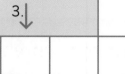
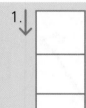

3 Circle the odd one out.

cake   eggs   mix   ape   bowl   pour

a–e

Read, then answer the questions.

Baking a cake

Today I am baking a cake for my brother.
He loves cherry chocolate.
I take four eggs and mix everything
in a bowl. I pour it all into a cake tin.
I give it a little shake.
I can frost it when it is baked.

1 Who is the cake for?

a me b my brother c my sister

2 What kind of cake is it?

a cherry b chocolate c cherry chocolate

3 I need _____ eggs.

a two b four c six

4 What happens after I shake the cake tin?

a It goes in the oven. b I drop it. c It goes in the bin.

5 What color frosting would you use?

_____

I finished this lesson online.	This egg hatched.	I can read and write: a–e words.	I can read

1 Join the puzzle pieces. ✏️ Write the words.

f r

a c e

l sp

_____

_____

_____

_____

2 Circle the **ace** words.

place   rate   cape   face   space

made   lace   pace   wave   race

3 Circle the rhyming words in each row.

race   ride   track   pace   face

bake   cake   save   take   plate

mane   mate   tape   cane   plane

4 Color the correct word. ✗ Cross out the wrong word.

Sam and Jazz have a (rate) (race).

You have a big smile on your (face) (lace).

Can you see the moon up in (spade) (space).

ace

1 Trace and write the words.

into

know

along

2 (Circle) **yes** or **no**.

Do you know who Sam the ant is?   **yes no**

Do you know your name?   **yes no**

Do you know your birthday?   **yes no**

Do you know the time?   **yes no**

3 Color **into** red, **along** yellow.

(into) (in) (on) (along) (song) (into)

(along) (a) (into) (long) (along) (under)

4 Complete the sentences.   into know along

I do not _____ your name.

We rode our bikes _____ the track.

We put the cake mix _____ the tin.

1 🖊 Match each word to a picture.

clouds

plane

stars

space

2 🖊 Draw a line under the correct sentence.

Baby Face wants to go up into space.

Baby Face wants to go under the zoo.

Baby Face gets onto an apple.

Baby Face gets onto a plane.

Baby Face flies high above the clouds.

Baby Face flies under the sea.

3 Color the correct word. ✗ Cross out the wrong word.

The plane flies (above) (higher) the clouds.

Baby face sees (mice) (stars) in the sky.

ace

Read, then answer the questions.

Baby Face in space

Baby Face wants to go to space.
She jumps into a plane. The plane is
nice, but it only flies to the clouds.
Baby Face needs a spaceship.
Icy Mice makes her one from cake,
rice, ripe tomatoes, and shoelaces.

1 Where does Baby Face want to go?
  a on holiday   **b** to a party   **c** up into space

2 How does she try to get there?
  a by car   **b** by plane   **c** by bike

3 Why does that not work?
  a It's too fast. **b** It only flies to the clouds. **c** It's too small.

4 What do the Icy Mice do?
  a make a plane   **b** bake a cake   **c** make a spaceship

5 What do they use?
  1. _____   2. _____
  3. _____   4. _____

I finished this
lesson online.

96

This egg
hatched.

I can read and write: ace
words, and other of a-e words.

I can read

Reading
eggs

Space race

vowels

The letters **a, e, i, o, u** are called **vowels**.
The other letters are called **consonants**.

1 Color the **vowels red** and the **consonants blue**.

d j b m e g t o

s x i u a y f l

p h v q c w n k

2 Which two consonants are missing. Write.

3 Say each word. Write the vowel.

a e i o u

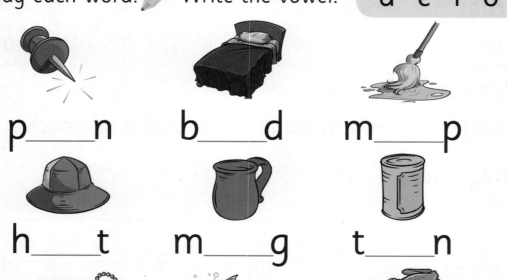

p___n   b___d   m___p   l___g

h___t   m___g   t___n   z___p

pl___g   f___sh   fr___g   fl___g

1 Make space compound words. Look at the picture. Color the correct word.

(dog) (suit)

space

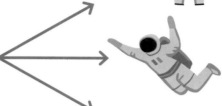

(walk) (tree)

(bee) (ship)

2 Use the compound words to complete the sentences.

An astronaut wears a _____.

A _____ flies in space.

Let's go for a _____
outside the spaceship.

3 Put the words in order. ✏ Write the sentence.

has This spacesuit. a astronaut

4 ✏ Write a sentence using these words.   astronaut spaceship

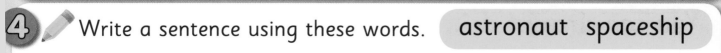

1 Match the action words to the pictures.

eat

draw

exercise

walk

play music

take photos

2 Color the **verbs**.

(astronaut) (spaceship) (walk) (eat) (play)

(exercise) (spacesuit) (ride) (fly) (photos)

3 Circle the correct word.

I am going to **eat** / **ear** all my food.

Riding a bike is a good way to **exercise** / **everywhere**.

Jazz likes to **bake** / **take** photos of flowers.

You can **draw** / **drink** a picture of my dog.

Shelley Shark is going to **wake** / **walk** to the shops.

Sam wants to **pale** / **play** music at his party.

vowels

Read, then answer the questions.

Life in Space

Eating
Astronauts sip drinks with a straw. They suck food from a pack.

Exercise
Astronauts exercise for 2 hours. Some like to run.

Clothes
Astronauts wear a spacesuit when they go outside.

Fun
Astronauts like to have fun. Some play music or take photos.

1 What things do you and astronauts do that are the same?

_____

_____

_____

2 What things do you and astronauts do that are **not** the same?

Astronauts	You
_____	_____
_____	_____
_____	_____

I finished this lesson online.	This egg hatched.	I can identify the vowels. I can read some space words.	I can read

vowel sounds

1 (Circle) the short vowel words in each row.

kite	bike	top	ride	hat	on
mice	bad	rake	rat	cake	maps
pip	nine	tin	lime	hit	bee
cage	hut	snake	pen	late	puppy

2 Add **e** to each short vowel word. ✏ Write. Match to a picture.

cap + e = _____

pin + e = _____

rob + e = _____

not + e = _____

3 Say the word. Join the letters. ✏ Write.

r → o   p   t
s   u   p → e   _____

k   e   t   e
c   i   t   r   _____

p   a   n   m
l   b   e   s   _____

vowel sounds

1 (Circle) the correct word.

 snak
snake

 cub
cube

 dim
dime

 tap
tape

 cut
cute

 can
cone

2 Join each word to the machine. ✏️ Write the new word.

hop
man
bit
plan
mad

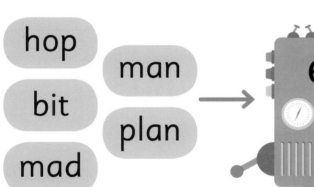 e

_____

_____

_____

_____

_____

3 Complete the word ladder. Change one letter at a time.

n

b

cu_____e

_____ube

tu_____e

_____une

t

c

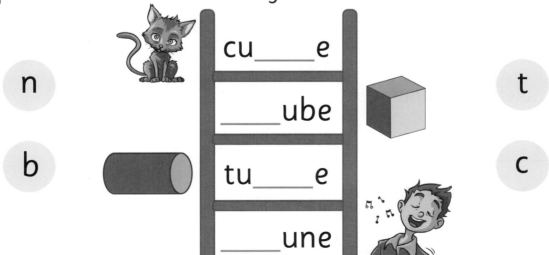

1 ✏️ Label each picture. **roll paint felt paper glue play dough**

g _____

f _____

p _____

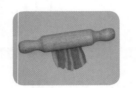

p _____

r _____

p _____

2 Color the correct word. ✗ Cross out the wrong word.

Sid can see a red (button) (butterfly) flying in the sky.

You can put all your toys in the (cardboard) (car park) box.

"I don't have any blue (pale) (paint) left," said Sam.

3 ✏️ Complete the sentences.   **paper Roll Glue**

_____ is very sticky.

You can draw and paint on _____ .

_____ the play dough to make it flat.

1 Read. Number 1 – 4 in the correct order.

Flatten the play dough with the rolling pin.

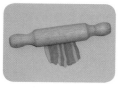

Cut out some fish shapes.

Roll the play dough into sausage shapes.

Line up all the play dough sausages.

2 What is the rolling pin for?

a to make play dough   **b** to flatten play dough

c to make sausage shapes

3 The sentences above tell you how to:

a make play dough.   **b** use a rolling pin.

c make fish from play dough.

4 What other animals can you make from play dough?

_____

I finished this lesson online.	This egg hatched.		I can read and write: short and long vowel sounds.	I can read

1 Color the words that end in the sound **ee**.

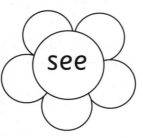

bee   ten   see   mate

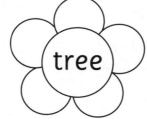
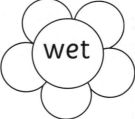

free   tree   wet   three

2 Use **ee** to make words.   Write each word. Read each word.

ee

m____t   n____d
k____p   d____p
f____t   s____n
b____n   w____k

3 Color the odd one out in each row.

see	bee	fee	beg	eel	tree
free	three	seed	said	seek	feed
feel	heel	whole	wheel	peel	steel

ending y

1 Color the words that end in **y**.

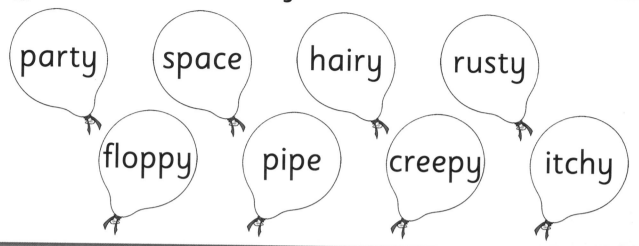

party space hairy rusty

floppy pipe creepy itchy

2 Join each word to the machine. Write the new word.

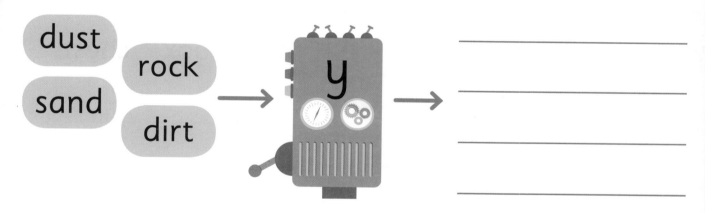

dust

rock

sand

dirt

y

_____

_____

_____

_____

3 How many sounds in each word?

f e e t
· — · ·
| 2 | 3 | 4 | 5 |

s m e l l y
· · · — ·
| 2 | 3 | 4 | 5 |

b e e
· — ·
| 2 | 3 | 4 | 5 |

b e n d y
· · · · ·
| 2 | 3 | 4 | 5 |

h a p p y
· · — ·
| 2 | 3 | 4 | 5 |

l u c k y
· · — ·
| 2 | 3 | 4 | 5 |

1 Match each word to a picture.

circus

box

chest

cage

tank

Vinny

2 Complete the sentences.

tank   box   chest

Vinny can escape from a _____.

Vinny can escape from a _____.

Vinny can escape from a _____.

3 Complete the crossword.
Use the picture clues to help you.

4. ↓

1. →

 1.

 2.

 3.

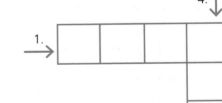

5. ↓

 4.

 5.

2. →

3. →

Reading **eggs** First Grade Workbook

ending y

Read, then answer the questions.

Tricky Vinny

Vinny works at the circus.

He can escape from anywhere.

"I am lucky," says Vinny.

"I can escape from this rusty, old cage and from that giant tank. It's all too easy for me!"

"I bet you can't escape from me," says Bendy Betty.

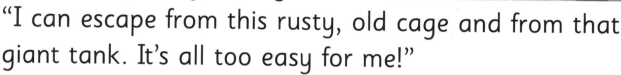

1 Where does Vinny work?

 a in a shop   **b** at the circus   **c** in a car park

2 What is his job?

 a He makes tanks.   **b** He drives car.
 c He escapes from things.

3 Why does Vinny say he is lucky?

 a His job is easy.   **b** His job is scary.   **c** His job is tricky.

4 Which is the opposite of easy?

 a soft   **b** hard   **c** lucky

5 Which word tells you about Betty?

 a Rusty   **b** Bendy   **c** Giant

I finished this lesson online.	This egg hatched.	I can read and write: ee words, and words ending in y.	I can read

1 Say the name of each picture. ✏️ Write in the missing sounds.

> age   ice   ch   th   sh   ike   ie   y

 b_____

 _____eese

 _____ark

 t_____

 m_____

 c_____

 itch____

3 _____ree

2 Color **soft c** words *yellow*, **soft g** words **red**.

circus	giant	age	icy
page	cent	mice	gym
Gemma	rice	circle	stage

3 ⬭Circle the correct word.

rack
rake
racke

gat
gaet
gate

1 Use the wheels to make words.  Write the words.

m b
ake
t l

d r
ice
m l

t c
ape
gr sh

_____ _____ _____

_____ _____ _____

_____ _____ _____

_____ _____ _____

2 Color **age** yellow, **ee** pink, **ime** green, **ake** blue.

(bee) (bake) (rage) (time) (Jake) (feel)

(cage) (lime) (keep) (dime) (stage) (take)

3 Sort the words into their word families. Write.

age	ee	ime	ake

4 Write the word in a box. 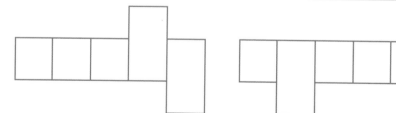 space rusty plane

1 Join each picture to a word.

celery   wave   gate   plane

giraffe   ape   game   bake

2 Unjumble the words.

c m e i

a v c e

p e t a

t l a e p

3 Color the correct word.

Vinny and Betty work at the (circle) (circus) .

You can (make) (made) a fish from play dough.

Astronauts can go for walks in (spade) (space) .

I keep my pet mice in a (cage) (stage).

1 ✏️ Complete the sentences.

> gelato   plane   ice   Giraffe   mice   chips

Icy Mice love to skate on _____.

Gemma Giraffe likes to eat _____.

Jet Set is a very fast _____.

Charlie likes to eat fish and _____.

Gemma _____ has very long legs.

The _____ can smell the cheese.

2 Match the sentences to the pictures.

I ride my bicycle in the park.

"I will bake this cake," said Jake the snake.

The astronaut is going for a spacewalk.

Vinny can escape from a chest.

I finished this lesson online.	This egg hatched.	I can read and write: a–e words, i–e words, and the words with y on the end.	I can read

1 Say the name of each picture. Color the word family.

(age) (ave) (ate) (ake) (ave) (ale) (ey) (ee)

2 (Circle) the rhyming words in each row.

mime	slime	pipe	time	lime	late
race	space	face	rip	lace	feet
wet	see	men	free	tree	bee

3 (Circle) the vowels in this sentence.

How many vowels did you find?

Sam is going up to space.

4 Make words with these letters.

a   o   d   y   t

2-letter word:

3-letter word:

5-letter word:

MAP 10 LESSONS 91 TO 100 # Quiz

5 Make compound words. Write the word. Match to a picture.

foot	ship	_____
space	brush	_____
shoe	ball	_____
tooth	lace	_____

6 Complete the sentences.

music above stars

The plane flies _____ the clouds.

Baby Face sees _____ in the sky.

Some astronauts like to play _____ in space.

7 Look at the picture. ✓ Check the matching sentence. ✗ Cross the wrong sentence.

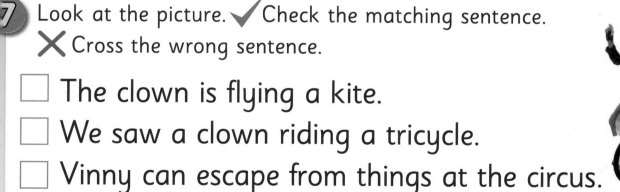

☐ The clown is flying a kite.

☐ We saw a clown riding a tricycle.

☐ Vinny can escape from things at the circus.

8 Write a sentence. Use the word **happy**.

_____

_____

Good Job!

YOU COMPLETED
MAP 10

YOU CAN:

☐ Read and write **soft c** words.

☐ Read and write **soft g** words.

☐ Read and write the **a–e** word family.

☐ Recognize the vowels **a, e, i, o,** and **u**.

☐ Read and write words that end in **y**.

☐ Read other words such as: **circus, unicycle, football, Saturday, rooster, mixing, astronaut, spaceship, escape,** and **tricky**.

☐ Read these books:

Reading eggs Level 3 91
Bicycles

Reading eggs Level 3 93
Gemma Giraffe

Reading eggs Level 3 97
Life in Space

Reading eggs Level 3 99
Can Vinny Escape?

Reading eggs First Grade Workbook

1 Find the words.

m	e	e	t	k	e	e	p	t	r	e	e
s	e	e	d	b	e	e	n	w	e	e	k
n	e	e	d	d	e	e	p	f	e	e	l
h	e	e	l	b	e	e	s	b	e	e	p
b	e	e	f	k	e	e	n	s	e	e	n

seen	beef	meet	heel	seed
deem	keep	feel	keen	been
week	need	tree	bees	beep

2 Complete the crossword. Use the picture clues to help you.

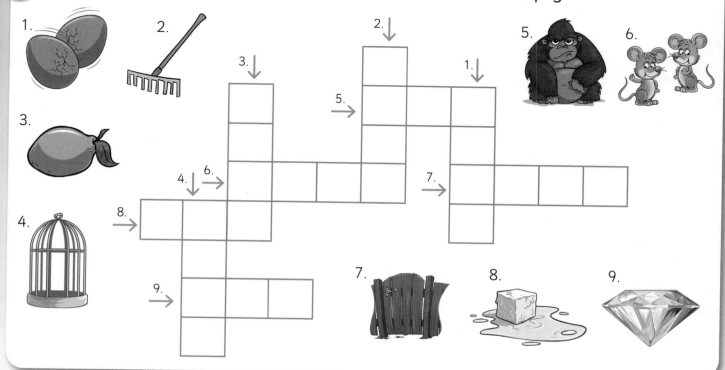

1 Color the **oo** words.

wood   book   Mom   cook   shop   Soot

2 Make **oo** words. ✏️ Write each word. Read each word.

c____k   t____k   l____k

b____k   f____t   w____l

Soot the cook says

oo

3 Say the name of each picture. Color its beginning sound, then its ending. ✏️ Write the word.

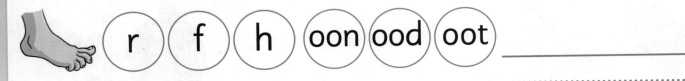

(r) (f) (h) (oon) (ood) (oot) _____

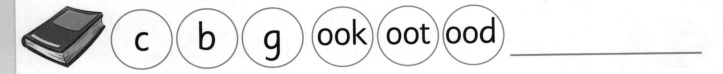

(c) (b) (g) (ook) (oot) (ood) _____

(w) (s) (t) (ood) (ook) (ool) _____

(h) (m) (l) (oof) (ood) (ook) _____

1 Join each word to a picture.

gelato

chocolate

banana

strawberry

lemon

piece

2 Complete each sentence.   strawberry   cook   cake

Soot the _____ loves cake.

Jake baked a chocolate _____ .

Gemma giraffe made a _____ gelato cake.

3 This banana cake is delicious!

What does **delicious** mean? ✓ the correct answer.

☐ It tastes yucky.

☐ It tastes yummy

☐ It tastes bad.

1 Read the clue. Write the word.

You get me from a sheep.
I am w_____.

I am brown and taste sweet.
I am ch_____.

I can bake cakes.
I am Soot the
c_____.

I am a yellow fruit.
I am a
b_____.

2 Color the correct word. ✗ Cross out the wrong one.

Soot the [cook] [book] baked a giant cake.

I love to eat really [sweet] [slice] fruit cake.

Sam had strawberries and [clean] [cream] for his dinner.

3 Use each word in a sentence.

chocolate _____

_____

today _____

_____

Read, then answer the questions.

How to make a banana cake

1 Put flour and sugar into a bowl.
2 Crack 3 eggs.
3 Add milk, eggs, and butter.
4 Mash 3 ripe bananas.
5 Add the bananas. Mix well.
6 Pour into a cake tin.
7 Bake until the cake is brown on top.

1 What is the text for?

a It tells a story.   **b** It tells how to bake.

2 Number 1–4 in the correct order.

☐ Mash the bananas.   ☐ Put flour and sugar into a bowl.
☐ Crack the eggs.   ☐ Add milk, eggs, and butter.

3 What does the word **ripe** mean?

a hard   **b** cold   **c** ready to eat

4 How do you know the cake is ready?

a It goes brown.   **b** It is ripe.   **c** It is mixed up.

5 What cake would you add to Soot's cookbook?

_____

I finished this lesson online.	This egg hatched.	I can read and write words with the soft oo sound.	I can read

1 Color the **oo** words.

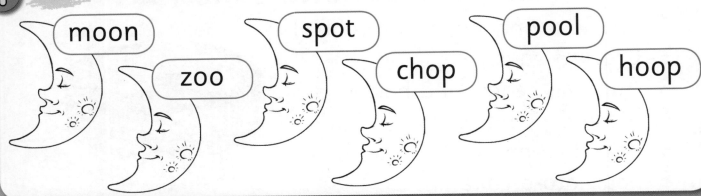

moon   zoo   spot   chop   pool   hoop

2 Use **oo** to make words. ✏️ Write each word.
Read each word.   Bunky Boo says

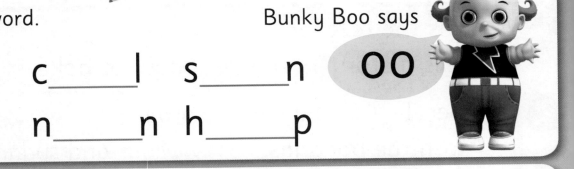

f____l   c____l   s____n   **oo**

t____l   n____n   h____p

3 Say the name of each picture. Color its beginning sound, then its ending. ✏️ Write the word.

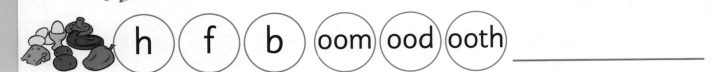 h   f   b   (oom)(ood)(ooth) _____

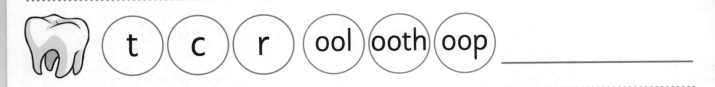 t   c   r   (ool)(ooth)(oop) _____

 cr   br   tr   (ool)(ook)(oom) _____

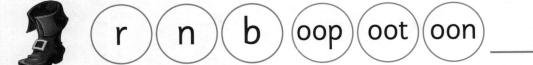 r   n   b   (oop)(oot)(oon) _____

long oo

1 Join each word to a picture.

spoon

cockatoo

baboon

kangaroo

tools

raccoon

2 Color the correct word. ✕ Cross out the wrong one.

A ⬚cockatoo⬚ ⬚baboon⬚ is a big, white bird.

A ⬚raccoon⬚ ⬚kangaroo⬚ can jump very far.

You can eat gelato with a ⬚tools⬚ ⬚spoon⬚.

3 ✏ Draw a baboon at the zoo eating goo with a spoon!

1 Read the clue. Write the word.

Lots of animals live here.

It is a z_____.

This word means the same as midday.

n_____

You use me to eat your soup.

I am a s_____.

A hammer, a saw, and a drill are all

t_____.

2 Color the correct word. ✗ Cross out the wrong one.

Sam eats his food with a [spade] [spoon] .

Jazz shoots the basketball into the [hoop] [hoot] .

Sid sweeps the floor with a [boom] [broom] .

I will meet you in the zoo at [soon] [noon] .

3 Write the words in the correct order.

kangaroos. can three I see

_____

_____

long oo

Read, then answer the questions.

Zoo goo

It is noon. Time for the cook
to bring her cookbook to the zoo.
"Boo!" says the kangaroo.
The cook makes really good goo.
She scoops goo onto the spoon.
"Cool!" says the raccoon.
The whole zoo loves good goo!

1 What time is it at the zoo?

  a bedtime   **b** noon   **c** bathtime

2 Who is coming to the zoo?

  a kangaroos   **b** cockatoos   **c** a cook

3 Who says "Boo!"?

  a the cook   **b** the kangaroo   **c** the raccoon

4 What do you know about the zoo?

  a it is really good   **b** it is really bad   **c** no one likes it

5 Why does the raccoon say "Cool!"?

  a he hates goo   **b** he loves goo   **c** he feels cold

I finished this lesson online.	This egg hatched.	I can read and write words with the long oo sound.	I can read

1 Put the letters through the word machine. Write the words you make.

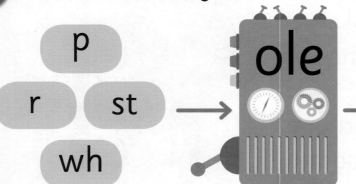

p

r   st

wh

→ ole →

_____

_____

_____

_____

2 Complete the **ole** words. Match to a picture.   m h p s

_____ ole

_____ ole

_____ ole

_____ ole

3 Color the **ole** words yellow.

hole   feel   mole   stole

role   pole   pale   sole

4 Put these words in alphabetical order.

pole   mole   sole   role

_____   _____   _____   _____

ole

1 Use the wheels to make words. ✏️ Write the words.

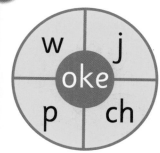

w   j
oke
p   ch

_____
_____
_____
_____

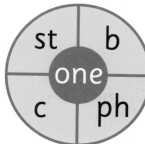

st   b
one
c   ph

_____
_____
_____
_____

2 (Circle) the rhyming words in each row.

woke   snake   spoke   joke   Jake

hole   help   stole   male   mole

phone   tone   pane   fine   bone

3 Color the word if it makes a **long o** sound.

(woke) (toe) (mole) (home) (cage)

(hole) (lots) (phone) (tone) (broke)

4 Color the correct word. ✕ Cross out the wrong one.

Moe the mole has a nice ring [tone] [zone] .

Tom the dog digs a big [pole] [hole]
for his bone.

1 Join each word to a picture.

mole

wombat

snake

kangaroo

bear

rabbit

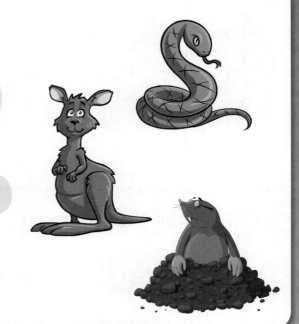

2 Read the clue. Write the word.

I like to dig holes.
I am Moe the

m_____.

I have a long body
and no legs. I am a

s_____.

I have fur and very
sharp claws. I am a

b_____.

I have long ears.
I love to eat carrots.
I am a _____.

3 Write the words in the correct order.

lost down hole. Moe phone that his

_____

_____

Read, then answer the questions.

Moe and the hole

Moe the mole lives in a hole. One day, poor Moe lost his phone down a hole. This hole was deep, dark, and scary. Who lived there? Was it a big, bad bear? Poor Moe. He did not like this hole!

1 Where does Moe live?

a in the park   **b** in a house   **c** in a hole

2 What has he lost?

a his hole   **b** his phone   **c** his rabbit

3 The hole is deep and _____ .

a down   **b** big   **c** dark

4 Moe thinks a _____ lives in this hole.

a snake   **b** bear   **c** mole

5 How does Moe feel about this hole?

a He is scared.   **b** He likes it.   **c** He wants to live there.

6 Write 3 words to describe a bear.

_____   _____   _____

I finished this lesson online.	This egg hatched.		I can read and write: ole words, and other o_e words.	I can read

1 Join the puzzle pieces. ✏ Write the words.

r h

o s e

n cl

_____

_____

_____

_____

2 Use the letters to make words.

v

r

j

_____ote
_____oke
_____ode

c

w

n

_____ote
_____oke
_____ode

3 Finish the sentences.

ose ote oke ode

Can you tell me a funny j_____.

Sam has a cold. He has a runny n_____.

Jazz r_____ her bike in the park.

I left a n_____ for Moe to give me a call.

1 Join each word to a picture.

flagpole

tadpole

ribbons

pond

stripes

seaweed

2 Color the correct word. ✗ Cross out the wrong one.

Coal the tadpole lives in a (stripes) (pond).

Every year, the (ribbons) (tadpoles) have a race around the pond.

Poor Tony got stuck in some (seaweed) (flagpole).

3 Put the words in the correct order. ✏ Write each sentence.

tadpole lives a Coal in pond. the

_____

race pond. The around tadpoles the

_____

1 Read. Match to a picture.

Today is the Pond Cup race.

Joan the tadpole has red ribbons and is bigger than Coal.

Coal swims through a hole in the rock.

Tiny Joe crosses the finishing line. Coal wins the Pond Cup.

2 Draw a picture to match each sentence.

The tadpoles race under the bubbly foam and over the blue stones.

Tony the tadpole has green spots. He gets tangled in the weed.

Reading eggs First Grade Workbook

o_e

Read, then answer the questions.

The Pond Cup Race

Tiny Joe is a little tadpole. Every year he hopes to win the Pond Cup Race. The other tadpoles are big and strong. They think Tiny Joe is a joke! Tiny Joe does not give up. He swims and swims and crosses the finish line first. Hooray for Tiny Joe!

1 What is Tiny Joe?

a a fish   b a tadpole   c an ant

2 What does he want to win?

a a running race   b a horse race   c a swimming race

3 When is the race?

a every year   b every day   c every week

4 Why do the others think Tiny Joe is a joke?

a he is funny   b he is too small   c he is a good swimmer

5 True or false? Tiny Joe comes last in the race.

a true   b false

I finished this lesson online.	This egg hatched.	I can read and write o_e words.	I can read

1 (Circle) the blobs if the word begins with the sound **bl**.

blow   blue   blaze   blew

bat   blob   lip

2 Make words. ✏️ Write each word.

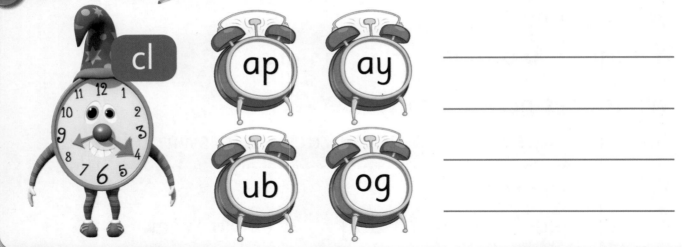

cl

ap   ay

_____

_____

ub   og

_____

_____

3 Join the jigsaw pieces together. ✏️ Write each word.

g r   o w   f r   e e

_____   _____

s w   a n   c r   i b

_____   _____

blends

1 Complete each word. ✏️ Draw its picture. | pl pl pl

u g

u m

a t e

2 Say the name of each picture. Color its beginning sound, then its ending. ✏️ Write the word.

(fr) (pl) (wh) (ere) (ane) (ine) _____

(br) (sm) (pl) (ush) (ate) (oke) _____

(cl) (gr) (sc) (arf) (ale) (ipe) _____

3 ✏️ Write each word in a box.

frog
slam
Clem
shell

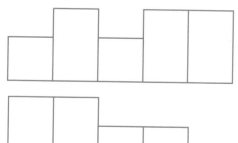

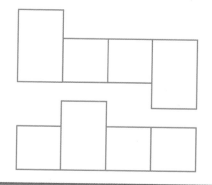

1 Join each word to a picture.

grub

crab

clam

swam

frog

crack

2 Use the words above to finish these sentences.

Clem the _____ clings to the rock.

The dinosaur egg started to _____ .

Me Be Fish _____ far out to sea.

The little green _____ jumped onto a leaf.

3 ✏ Write the words in the correct box.

whale   clam   slug   crab   grub   frog

lives by the sea	lives in the garden

blends

1 Complete the sentences. **slams   clam   fly**

Clem is a _____ .

"I want to _____ like a bird."

Clem's shell _____ shut.

2 ✏ Draw.

A fish tries to eat Clem the clam.

3 ✏ Write a sentence to match each picture.

_____

_____

_____

_____

I finished this lesson online.	This egg hatched.	I can read and write words with initial blends.	I can read
		☺	

1 Color the grubs green if the word begins with **gr**.

girl · grub · grow · grape · grip · goat · grab

2 Make words. ✏️ Write each word.

pr · op · am · ize · une

_____

_____

_____

_____

3 Make words that begin the same. Read the words.

br ick	**dr** ink	**sn** ail
_____ ag	_____ op	_____ ow
_____ oom	_____ ag	_____ ap
_____ ing	_____ ip	_____ ug

blends

1 ✏️ Write the words on the correct brick.

green
grub
tree
grab
trap
trip

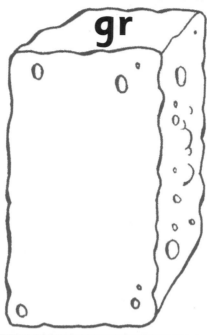

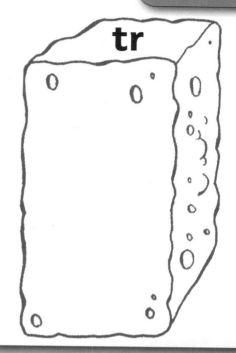

2 Use the wheels to make words. ✏️ Write the words.

ate | op
cr
ane | eep

_____
_____
_____
_____

ew | op
dr
ive | ag

_____
_____
_____
_____

3 Say the name of each picture. Color its beginning sound, then its ending. ✏️ Write the word.

 (tr) (pr) (gr) (awn) (ape) (ain) _____

 (tr) (pr) (gr) (awn) (ape) (ain) _____

 (tr) (pr) (gr) (awn) (ape) (ain) _____

1 ✏️ Complete the sentences.

br   dr   Fr   cr

_____ogfish is _____ave.
He will not _____y when
he hears the big _____um.

2 ✏️ Write a sentence to match each picture.

3 ✏️ Draw

a grotty grub grinning.

a green tree frog creeping
up a tree trunk.

blends

Read, then answer the questions.

Fred

Fred is a big, green tree frog.
He lives on a leaf. Fred likes to
munch and crunch on grotty grubs.
The grotty grub tries to trick Fred.
But Fred grabs the grub and traps him.
Mmmm... a grotty grub for lunch!

1. What color is Fred?

   a brown   b yellow   c green

2. Where does Fred live?

   a on a leaf   b in a pond   c on a brick

3. What does Fred eat?

   a fish   b ants   c grotty grubs

4. The grotty grub tricks Fred because _____.

   a he wants to play   b he thinks he may get eaten

   c he wants Fred to be his friend

5. What's Fred having for lunch today?

   _____

I finished this lesson online.	This egg hatched.	I can read and write words with initial blends.	I can read

1 Color the words with **ea**.

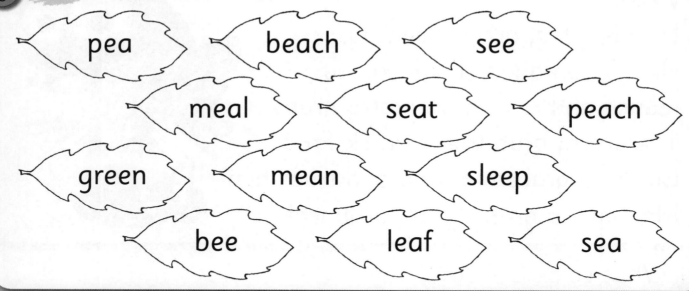

pea   beach   see

meal   seat   peach

green   mean   sleep

bee   leaf   sea

2 Make **ea** words. Write each word. Read each word.

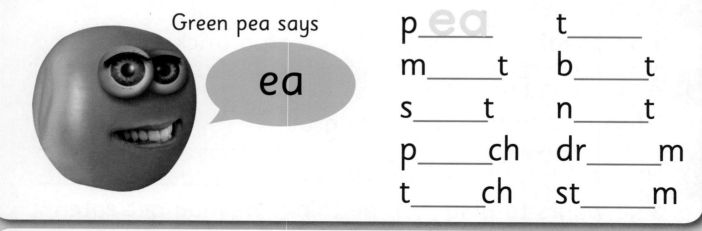

Green pea says

ea

p_ea_   t____
m____t   b___t
s____t   n___t
p____ch   dr____m
t____ch   st____m

3 Say the word. Join the letters. Write.

b   a   a   f
l   e   e   n   

b   a   a   f
l   e   e   n

1 Complete the **long e** words. Match to a picture.

ee   ea

p_____s

dr_____m

tr_____

wh_____l

2 Color **ea** words **red**, **ee** words **green**.

beach   feet   queen   seat   tea

feel   beak   beep   fine   cream

3 Sort the words into their word families.

ea	ee

4 Circle the odd one out.

me   see   dream   bead   pet   feet   peach

1 Join each word to a picture.

pea

peach

dream

leaf

beach

beast

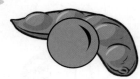

2 Read the clue. ✏️ Write the word.

I am small, round, and green. You can eat me.
I am a p_____.

I am a big, scary monster.
I am a b_____.

I am next to the sea. I have sand.
I am a b_____.

I am green. I grow on trees.
I am a l_____.

3 ✏️ Write the word in a box.

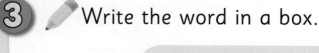

screams   leave   feels

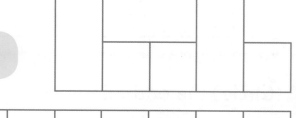

Read, then answer the questions.

Little pea

The little green pea is at the beach.
She sees the sea and eats a peach.
Soon the little pea falls asleep.
She has a dream that makes her scream.
She sees a seal. The mean seal eats the little green pea.
Lucky for her it's just a dream.

1 Number 1–4 in the correct order.

☐ The pea wakes up.

☐ The pea sees the sea at the beach.

☐ The mean seal eats the pea.

☐ The little pea falls asleep and dreams.

2 Why does the little pea's dream make her scream?

a The seal eats her.　　**b** The seal falls asleep.

c She doesn't like the sea.

3 Why is the little pea lucky?

a She sits on a leaf.　　**b** She sees a seal.

c Her dream is not real.

I finished this lesson online.	This egg hatched.	I can read and write ea, and ee words.	I can read
			A Green Pea

1 Join the puzzle pieces. Write the words.

J   d

u n e

pr   t

_____

_____

_____

_____

2 Use the letters to make words.

m
c   t

_____ube
_____ute
_____ule

fl   r
t

_____ube
_____ute
_____ule

3 Circle the correct word.

dune
dime

cube
cape

meal
mule

flute
flea

table
tube

prune
pond

u_e

① Join the word to Duke if it makes a **long u** sound.

cute

pet

tube

cube

flute

store

tune

June

chute

rice

plate

prune

② ✏ Sort the **long u** words into word families.

ube	ute	une

③ Complete the sentences.   cube   flute   cute

Duke liked to play the _____.
The Icy mice jumped onto a _____.
The _____ little Catty cakes had big ears.

1 Match each verb to a picture.

hop

run

fly

play

dance

snooze

2 Join each verb to the past tense.

hop	run	fly	play	dance	snooze

played	hopped	ran	snoozed	flew	danced

3 Choose the correct word for each sentence.

danced   hopped   snooze   play

Duke the June bug like to _____ the flute.

Red Rabbit _____ around his cage.

The Icy Mice _____ to the tune.

The pets felt sleepy and had a _____.

Reading eggs First Grade Workbook

u_e

Read, then answer the questions.

Duke's pet

Duke the June bug went to the pet store.
He saw a rabbit and some blue birds.
Duke got out his flute. He played a tune.
The Icy Mice danced to his tune.
The other pets snoozed.
"These mice are perfect pets!" said Duke.

① Where did Duke go?

_____

② Why did he go there?

_____

③ Write 2 animals he saw in the store.

_____

④ Which pet did Duke pick?

_____

⑤ Why did Duke choose this pet?

_____

I finished this lesson online.	This egg hatched.	I can read and write u_e words.	I can read
		☺	Duke Plays the Flute

1 Color the words with **er**.

her	far	germ	tiger	farm
paper	were	was	herb	card
tower	verb	Baxter	dear	better

2 Make **er** words. Write each word. Read each word.

Baxter the badger says

er

help_____   bigg_____
broth_____   bett_____
sist_____   farm_____
badg_____   play_____

3 Circle the correct word.

cleaner   plumber   ranger   baker
farmer   teacher   builder   gardener

4 Write the sentence in the correct order.

Baxter   be   Today   will   builder.   a

_____

_____

1 Make a rainbow word. Copy the word.

better

2 Join the letters to make **better**.   Circle **better**.

b	d	t	o	n
a	e	m	t	f
c	a	n	e	g
d	e	w	i	r

better	been
before	better
badger	builder
batter	better
better	brother

3 Make words with these letters.   t e e t b

r

2-letter word: ◯ ◯

4-letter word: ◯ ◯ ◯ ◯

6-letter word: ◯ ◯ ◯ ◯ ◯ ◯

1 Join each word to a picture.

| water |
| plumber |
| cleaner |
| gardener |
| builder |
| badger |

2 Read the clue. Write the word.

I fix broken pipes.
I am a
p_____.

I look after plants.
I am a
g_____.

This word is the opposite of **hotter**.
c_____

This word is the opposite to **sister**.
b_____

3 Add **er**. Write the words you make.

play

mix   sing

farm

er

_____

_____

_____

_____

Reading eggs First Grade Workbook

er

1 ✏ Complete the sentences.

better badger plumber

Baxter the _____ can fix the leaky faucet.

"Today I will be a _____," he said.

Baxter put a bigger and _____ faucet

on the sink.

2 Answer the questions.

Who is Baxter?

a a builder **b** a badger **c** a mole

Another word for **leaky** is _____ .

a dry **b** cold **c** dripping

What kind of faucet does Baxter now have?

a better **b** shiny **c** smaller

3 ✏ Write a sentence using Baxter's word.

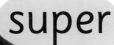

super _____

_____

I finished this lesson online.	This egg hatched.	I can read and write words ending in er.	I can read
 109			Bigger Better Baxter

1 Join the jigsaw pieces together. Write each word.

d r · i p   t tr · e e

_____   _____

g r · o w   f l · a t

_____   _____

2 Say the word for each picture. Write the beginning sound.

_____ower
_____ap
_____ag

_____ock
_____ap
_____ug

3 Color the plum if the word begins with **pl**.

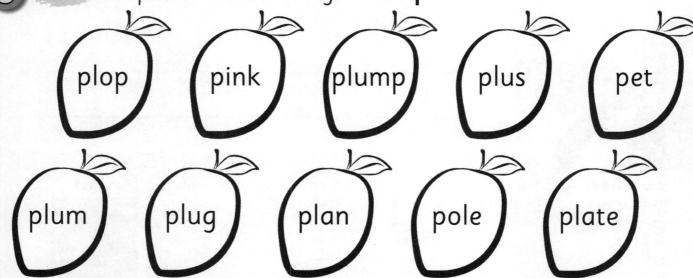

plop   pink   plump   plus   pet

plum   plug   plan   pole   plate

blends

1 Join the blends to the endings to make the words.

 cl

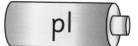 pl

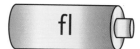 fl

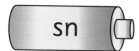 sn

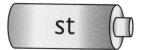 st

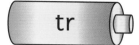 tr

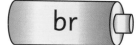 br

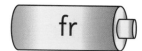 fr

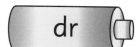 dr

ag

ail

ock

ug

og

ar

ink

ee

oom

2 Use the wheels to make words. Write the words.

op | at
fl
an | ood

_____
_____
_____
_____

ow | ab
gr
een | in

_____
_____
_____
_____

 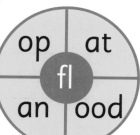

1 Join each word to a picture.

squishy

crunchy

dry

strong

soft

pretty

2 Complete the sentences.   **strong crunchy pretty**

The rabbit ate a _____ carrot.

A _____ flower grew in the ground.

Flossy the plum tree had a big,

_____ trunk.

3 Which word

is the opposite of **wet**?   _____

is the opposite of **ugly**?   _____

means the same as **squishy**?_____

Read, then answer the questions.

Flossy

Flossy was a plum tree.
Flossy's trunk was brown and strong.
Her flowers were white and pretty.
Flossy's leaves were green and glossy.

1 What was Flossy?

a a plum   **b** a flower   **c** a plum tree

2 Flossy's _____ was brown.

a leaves   **b** trunk   **c** plums

3 What is the opposite of **strong**?

a little   **b** dry   **c** weak

4 Which 2 words tell you about Flossy's flowers?

1. _____   2. _____

5 What is another word for **glossy**?

a green   **b** shiny   **c** soft

6 Flossy feels happy and well.   **a** True   **b** False

1 Say the name of each picture. Color the beginning sound.

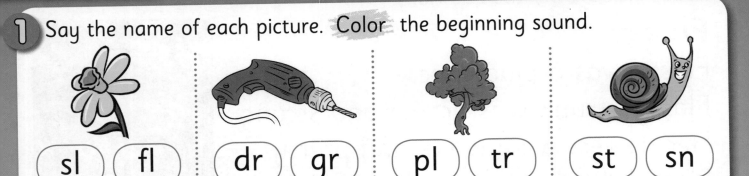

| sl | fl | dr | gr | pl | tr | st | sn |

2 Circle the rhyming words in each row.

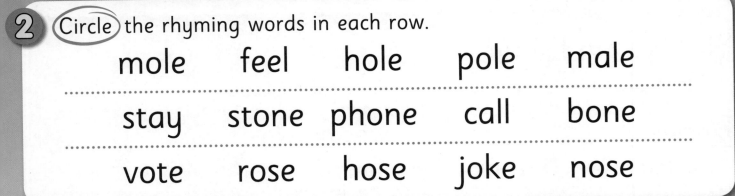

| mole | feel | hole | pole | male |

| stay | stone | phone | call | bone |

| vote | rose | hose | joke | nose |

3 Read. Circle the oo words.

Soot the cook went to the zoo. He saw a baboon playing in a pool. Soot took out his wooden spoon and ate some goo.

Color the **long oo** words **red**, **short oo** words yellow.

4 Write the word in a box.   peach June spoon

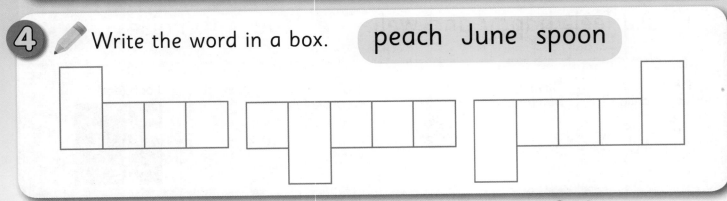

MAP 11 LESSONS 91 TO 110

Quiz

5 Join Baxter to **er** words.

hotter

helper

brother

little

greener

colder

build

sister

6 Color the correct word.

Little sweet pea likes to eat a (beach)(peach).

Flossy the tree has glossy (leaves)(meals).

When I fall asleep I always (stream)(dream).

7 Complete the sentences.

use cute tune

Look at that _____ little puppy!

She can play a _____ on her flute.

You can _____ my pencils.

8 Look at the picture. ✔ Check the matching sentence.
✗ Cross the wrong sentences.

☐ The Icy Mice danced to Duke's tune.

☐ Clem the Clam clings to a rock.

☐ Gemma Giraffe made a gelato cake.

★ Awesome!

YOU COMPLETED

MAP 11

YOU CAN:

- [ ] Read and write **oo** words.
- [ ] Read and write **o_e** and **u_e** words.
- [ ] Read and write words ending in **er**.
- [ ] Read and write **ea** words.
- [ ] Hear **initial blends** and read and write new words.
- [ ] Read words such as: **excited, ground, together, friends, grotty, scary,** and **perfect**.
- [ ] Read these books:

Reading eggs Level 3 101

Soot's Cook Book

Reading eggs Level 3 104

The Pond Cup

Reading eggs Level 3 107

A Green Pea

Reading eggs Level 3 110

The Plum Tree

1 Crack the code. Answer the question.

h	m	n	l	a	i	v	o	e	c
✿	★	▲	✔	♥	■	◆	●	☾	☺

☺ ♥ ▲ ♥   ★ ● ✔ ☾

✔ ■ ◆ ☾   ■ ▲   ♥

✿ ● ✔ ☾   **?**   Color the correct answer.

(yes)   (no)

2 ✏ Draw

| two green peas on a leaf by the sea. | Gemma Giraffe's icy gelato cake. |

blends

1 Color the glass if the word starts with **gl**.

glass glad grub glue

gate glum good glove

2 Join Brad the Crab to each shell. ✏️ Write each word.

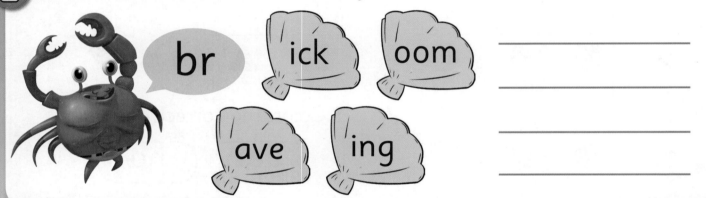

br

ick   oom

ave   ing

_____

_____

_____

_____

3 ✏️ Write the words on the correct truck.

track
truck
crash
try
crab
crown

cr

tr

Reading **eggs** First Grade Workbook

blends

1 Join the jigsaw pieces together. ✏️ Write each word.

d r o p   s n a i l

_____   _____

c l a p   s c a r f

_____   _____

2 Say the word for each picture. ✏️ Write the beginning sound.

_____ab
_____op
_____ack

_____ar
_____op
_____age

3 Say the name of each picture. Color its beginning sound, then its ending. ✏️ Write the word.

br cr tr ad uck ing _____

sl gl pl ove ab own _____

br tr cl ap ack ick _____

1 Match each word to a picture.

crab

truck

track

tree

cry

friends

2 Read the clue. ✏️ Write the word.

I have branches and green leaves.
I am a t_____.

Trains can travel on me.
I am a t_____.

I have lots of wheels. I can carry heavy things.
I am a t_____.

I live in the sand.
I have ten legs.
I am a c_____.

3 ✏️ Put the words in order to make each sentence.

the walked the Brad up track. crab

_____

had the three crab friends. Brad

_____

blends

Read, then answer the questions.

Brad the crab

Brad is a crab. He lives on a beach by the sea. Brad wants to go on a trip to see the world. Brad cannot drive a truck. Sometime Brad has a bit of a cry. Brad has three friends.

1 True or false?

Brad lives on a farm.	a true	b false
Brad is a clam.	a true	b false
Brad wants to see the world.	a true	b false
Brad has friends.	a true	b false

2 How are you and Brad **not** the same?

_____

_____

_____

_____

3 How are you and Brad the same?

_____

_____

_____

_____

I finished this lesson online.

This egg hatched.

I can read and write words using blends.

I can read

Brad the Crab

1. Clap the syllables as you say each word.
   Write each word in the correct box.

cup	happy	eating	cake
flower	hotter	crab	slam

1 clap

_____

_____

_____

2 claps

_____

_____

_____

2. Color words with one syllable **red**, 2 syllables yellow.

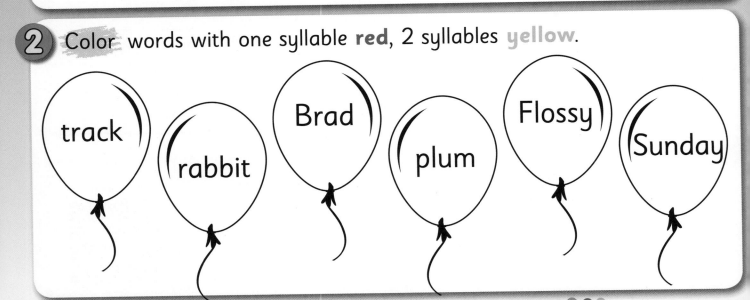

track

rabbit

Brad

plum

Flossy

Sunday

syllables

1 Make compound words. ✏ Write the word.

  base bow _____

  rain ball _____

 space pole _____

 tad ship _____

2 ✏ Write the missing syllable to complete each word.

rot er bit on ing

 flow_____

 car_____

 lem_____

 rab_____

 wat_____

 eat_____

 ex_____cise

 sleep_____

3 Say the word. (Circle) the syllables. ✏ Write the word.

 1 2 3 _____

 1 2 3 _____

1 Match each picture to a word.

food

water

exercise

sleep

home

clothes

2 Read the clue. ✎ Write the word.

You can drink this from a glass.

I am _____.

You can live in me.

I am a _____.

When you run, jump, or walk.

I am _____.

You do this when you close your eyes.

I am _____.

3 Color the correct word. ✗ Cross out the wrong one.

When I am hungry, I need to eat (feed) (food).

Shelley got new (clothes) (cloths) at the shop.

Sam had a big drink of (wetter) (water).

1 Match the sentences to the pictures.

Exercise helps us to live and grow.

Food helps us to grow strong.

We need a home to live in.

Sleep helps my body to stay healthy.

2 Answer the questions.

What exercise do you like to do?

_____

_____

What food do you like to eat?

_____

_____

I finished this lesson online.	This egg hatched.	I can break words into syllables.	I can read

1 Say the words. Join them to a critter.

thank

nk

ck

sink

lick

stick

clock

ink

tank

pack

2 ✏ Complete each word.

lk nd ng st nt ft

gi_____

sa_____

mi_____

a_____

gho_____

go_____

3 Say the name of each picture. Color its beginning, middle, and ending sound. ✏ Write the word.

st sk u a nd nk _____

st sh u a mp nd _____

d b o e il lt _____

end blends

---

1 Use the wheels to make words. ✏️ Write the words.

sku pi
nk
Fra sti

_____

_____

_____

_____

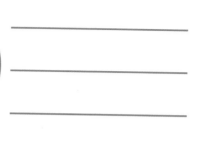

wa si
lk
mi ta

_____

_____

_____

_____

---

2 Use the letters to make words.

nd ng nk

ri _____
ta _____
be _____

lk mp ft

le _____
ju _____
mi _____

---

3 Say the word. Join the letters. ✏️ Write.

st   e   mp
sh → a   np

_____

gr   i   nk
dr   o   lk

_____

g   u   st
j   i   ft

_____

1 Join each word to a picture.

skunk

milk

pink

sink

drink

stink

2 Read the clue. Write the word.

I am furry. I have four legs and I can smell bad!
I am a sk_____ .

I am made by cows. You can drink me.
I am m_____ .

You can fill me with water and wash the dishes.
I am a s_____ .

I am a color. I am made when you mix red and white.
I am p_____ .

3 Color the correct word. ✗ Cross out the wrong one.

This is Frank the (stink) (skunk). Frank likes to (drink) (drift) pink milk. Frank sits on the (sang) (sand). He (gulps) (stings) the pink drink.

Read, then answer the questions.

Frank's pink milk

Frank the skunk and Tink the flamingo like to drink pink milk. They see a glass of pink milk on the sink. They both want it! Frank is a stinky skunk. Tink smells the stink and runs away.

1 What is Frank?

　a a flamingo　　**b** a drink　　**c** a skunk

2 What color is Tink?

　a white　　**b** pink　　**c** red

3 What do Frank and Tink both want?

　a milk　　**b** water　　**c** to play

4 Why does Tink run away?

　a she sees a friend　**b** she is hungry　**c** Frank is too smelly

5 Who do you think gets to drink pink milk?

_____

I finished this lesson online.	This egg hatched.	I can read and write words with end blends.	I can read

oa

1 Color the boats that have an **oa** sound.

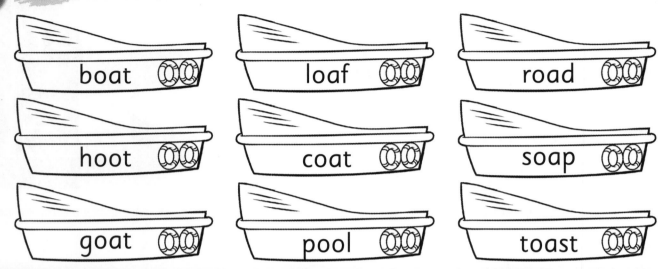

boat   loaf   road

hoot   coat   soap

goat   pool   toast

2 Make **oa** words. Write each word. Read each word.

Floaty Boat says

oa

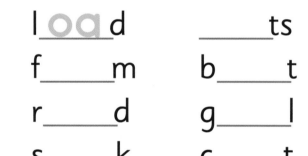

l **oa** d   ____ts

f____m   b____t

r____d   g____l

s____k   c____t

3 Say the name of each picture. Color its beginning, middle, and ending sound. Write the word.

  (t) (b) (o) (oa) (ts) (st) _____

(s) (g) (oa) (ao) (f) (t) _____

 (s) (c) (oo) (oa) (p) (b) _____

1 Join each word to a picture.

oats

coast

road

toast

soap

float

2 Complete the sentences.

float   toast   oats   soap

I ate _____ with honey for breakfast.

Wash your hands with _____ and water.

Boats can _____ on the sea.

I would like a bowl of hot _____ .

3 Join a word from the box to make a new word. Write.

coat   hat   boat

 sail + _____ = _____

 rain + _____ = _____

 top + _____ = _____

1 Complete the sentences.

> goat   oats   boat   soak   toast

The goat had a _____ in some soap.

Do you want toast or _____?

I cannot miss that _____!

He made some _____ .

The _____ missed the boat.

2 Match each sentence to a picture.

Oats the goat had a foamy soak.

"My goal today is to get onto a boat," says Oats.

The goat want to eat toast and oats.

3 Write a sentence to match the picture.

_____

_____

Read, then answer the questions.

Oats the goat

Today, Oats the goat must catch a boat.
He has a nice soak, then he eats toast and
oats. Next, he finds his raincoat and goes out.
He takes the Coast Road to catch his boat,
but Oats is too late. He missed his boat.

1 When must Oats catch a boat?

   a tomorrow   **b** today   **c** Tuesday

2 Number 1–4 in the correct order.

  ☐ Oats misses his boat.

  ☐ Oats finds his raincoat.

  ☐ Oats has a soak in the bath.

  ☐ Oats takes the Coast Road.

3 What does the goat eat for breakfast?

   a toast and butter   **b** oats and milk   **c** toast and oats

4 What do you eat for breakfast?

_____

I finished this lesson online.	This egg hatched.	I can read and write oa words.	I can read

1 Color the **ir** words.

car   card   skirt   bird

swirl   girl   trim   stir

2 Make **ir** words. Write each word. Read each word.

Twirly Bird says

ir

f_____   th_____d

sk_____t   ch_____p

f_____st   c_____cus

3 Write the word on the correct tower.

herb   fern
curl   burn
hurt   turn
germ   her

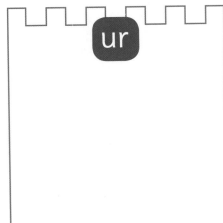 ur

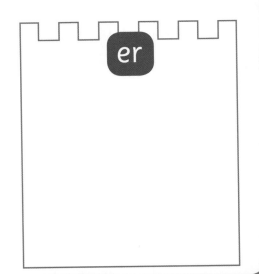 er

1 Join Shelley shark to the **ar words**.

park

scarf

storm

dark

farm

chair

cart

shark

2 Color **or** words **red**.

horn   short   yard   fork   germ

skirt   form   car   corn   snort

3 Complete each word.

ur   er   ar   ir   or

c___t   g___m   sk___t   c___n   n___se

4 Write the word in a box.

fork   scar   surf

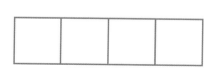  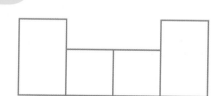

1 Join each word to a picture.

seeds

seedlings

soil

water

sunlight

trees

2 Read the clue. Write the word.

You plant me. I grow into seedlings.

I am s_____ .

I come out of a tap. You cannot live without me.

I am w_____.

We can grow tall. We have branches and leaves.

We are t_____ .

I am sometimes called dirt or earth. Seeds grow in me.

I am s_____ .

3 Write the words in the correct order.

soil and grow. need to Flowers live

_____

_____

Read, then answer the questions.

Plants

Plants need things to help them grow healthy and strong. They need soil to grow in. They need water to drink. They also need lots of sunlight to grow.

1 ✏️ Complete the table.

Plants	
need ✓	**do not need** ✗

cake
water
soil
wool
sunlight
milk

2 ✏️ Draw a picture of a plant.

3 What kind of plant is it?

_____

4 What helps a plant to grow?

_____

_____

_____

_____

igh

1 Join the **igh** words to Nighty night light.

high

knight

sing

fight

Bedtime Stories

skip

night

sigh

like

2 Join the puzzle pieces. ✏ Write the words.

l   s

m   i   g   h   t

r   t

_____

_____

_____

_____

3 Use the wheel to make words. ✏ Write the words.

n   f

ight

br   fl

_____   _____

_____   _____

4 ✏ Label.

kn_____

⌐n_____

igh

1 Join the two words together. ✏ Write each new word.

moon + light = _____

good + night = _____

star + light = _____

sun + light = _____

2 Join each picture to a word.

moonlight

goodnight

starlight

sunlight

3 Read the clue. ✏ Write the word.

You say it when you are going to bed.

It is _____ .

You can see this in the daytime.

It is _____ .

This is the light that comes from the stars.

It is _____ .

This is the shiny, white light of the moon.

It is _____ .

1 ✏ Complete the sentences.

> Goodnight   high   Bird   night   daytime

"I like to fly," said _____.

"I can fly _____ in the sky," said Bat.

Bird can fly in the _____.

Bat can fly all _____.

"_____," said Bird.

2 ✏ Read the sentences above. Answer the questions.

Who can fly at night?

_____

Who can fly in the daytime?

_____

What do you think Bird does at night?

_____

3 ✏ Write a sentence using Bat's word.

moonlight

_____

_____

This is a fact book.

Contents	Page
Chapter 1 Kinds of bats	2
Chapter 2 What bats eat	4
Chapter 3 How bats fly	6
Chapter 4 Where bats live	8

Read and answer the questions.

1 What is this book about?

_____

2 How many chapters are there?

_____

3 What will page 4 tell you?

_____

4 What is chapter 1 called?

_____

5 Which chapter tells you about where bats live?

_____

6 Which chapter tells you how bats move their wings?

_____

I finished this lesson online.	This egg hatched.	I can read and write igh words.	I can read

1 Match each common noun to its picture.

lion

drink

paw

thorn

net

rope

2 Color Roary's common nouns.

mice		net
cake		and
much		rope
thorn		friends

3 ✏ Write 2 common nouns that start with:

a	m	s

1 Match each proper noun to its picture.

Shelly

Jazz

Sam

Baxter

2 Write the nouns in the correct boxes. Hint! Look for the capital letters.

Monday
bird
Charlie
leaf
tooth
Africa
stick
July

common nouns

proper nouns

3 Write 2 proper nouns that start with:

B	T	J

Reading **eggs** First Grade Workbook

247

1 Complete the sentences.

net   cake   friends   drink

Roary wanted an icy cold _____.

Roary got caught in a _____.

Catty was baking a _____.

"It's good to have _____!"

2 Give each proper noun a capital letter.

charlie likes to swing in the trees.

I went to a party on sunday.

reggie loves to read books.

My friend tom lives in kansas.

Color a star each time you write a capital. ☆ ☆ ☆ ☆ ☆

3 Write a sentence using Roary's word.

lion

_____

_____

nouns

Read, then answer the questions.

Best friends

Roary the lion got a thorn stuck in his paw.
Then he got stuck in a big net.
The little mice came to help him.
They chewed the rope until Roary was free.
Now, Roary and the mice are best friends.

1 Who is Roary?

_____

2 What happened first to Roary?

_____

3 What happened next to Roary?

_____

4 Who helped Roary?

_____

5 What did the mice do?

_____

6 How do you think Roary felt?

_____

I finished this lesson online.	This egg hatched.	I can recognize common and proper nouns.	I can read
		⊙‿⊙	

1 Make **or** words. Write each word. Read each word.

Spiny porcupine says

or

c_____k   st_____m

t_____n   th_____n

f_____k   st_____k

2 Color **or** words orange, **ur** words **purple**.

(turn)   (short)   (worn)   (burn)   (fork)

(curly)   (sort)   (churn)   (corn)   (storm)

3 Sort the words into their word families.

or	ur

4 Write the word in a box.

form   corn   thorn

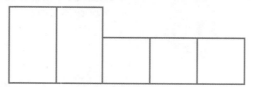

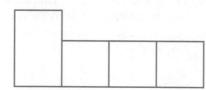

1  Trace.   Write.

   ore   ore

2 Color the **ore** words.

(bore) (snore) (cloud) (card) (chore) (store)

(care) (wore) (poor) (more) (shore) (core)

3 Put the letters through the word machine. Write the words.

sn

sh

sc

 ore →

_____

_____

_____

4 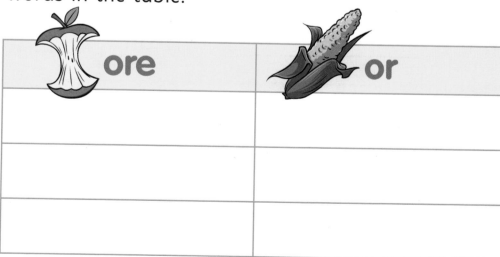 Write the words in the table.

corn
core
bore
horn
storm
chore

ore	or

1 Match each picture to a word.

T-shirt

raincoat

sweater

long pants

shirt

shorts

2 Read the clue. ✏️ Write the word.

Wear me in the rain to keep you dry.
I am a _____ .

I have short sleeves and a round neck.
I am a _____ .

I have long sleeves.
I am made from wool.
I am a _____ .

I am long and keep your legs warm.
I am _____ .

3 ✏️ Write the words in the correct order.

raincoats   boots.   We   and   rain   wore

_____

_____

ore

Read, then answer the questions.

Weather chart

Day	Weather	
Monday	sunny and hot	
Tuesday	cloudy and cool	
Wednesday	rainy and wet	
Thursday	windy and cold	
Friday	sunny and warm	

1 What was the weather like on Wednesday?

_____

2 Which day was cloudy and cool?

_____

3 On which day did it rain?

_____

4 What would you wear on Monday?

_____

5 What would you wear on Tuesday?

_____

6 On which day would you need a raincoat?

_____

I finished this lesson online.	This egg hatched.	I can read and write ore words.	I can read
 (118)		☺	Clothes

verbs

1 Match the animal to the correct verb. Color the verb.

- fly
- hop
- crawl

- swoop
- wriggle
- creep

- swim
- run
- fly

- pounce
- creep
- stomp

- dance
- pounce
- fly

- trot
- run
- swim

2 Color the action verbs.

 dance
 skate
 T-shirt
 run
 catch
 walk

 hop
 glasses
 throw
 jump
 feet
kick

3 Write the verb that matches each body part.

run   nod   tap   clap

 head

hands

 feet

 legs

_____   _____   _____   _____

254

Reading eggs First Grade Workbook

verbs

1 Match each saying verb to its picture.

shout

whisper

ask

giggle

2 Cross out the word **says**. Choose a better verb from the list.

hisses   barks   roars   asks

"What's the time?" says Tick tock clock. _____

"I love to bake cakes," says Jake the snake. _____

"Let's go and play!" says Tom the dog. _____

"Vroom, vroom!" says Fast As the racing car.

_____

3 Write the verbs in the correct places.

chat fly say tell lick dig sigh drink

 saying verbs

 action verbs

_____   _____

_____   _____

_____   _____

verbs

1 Match.

To stick to, or hold on tight.	flap
To make a high sound or cry.	wriggle
To rush down, or pounce.	swoop
To move wings up and down.	squeal
To twist or turn.	cling

2 ✏ Complete each sentence.

walks   pounces   clings   flaps

Roary the lion runs and _____ on his food.

Coco the starfish _____ onto rocks with her feet.

Brad the crab _____ sideways on his eight legs.

Blue bird _____ his wings to fly.

3 Color the right verb. ✖ Cross out the wrong one.

"I live in a lovely nest," builds sings Blue wing.

"Let's scribble a picture!" laughs draws Scribble stick.

"Shh! I need a little nap," sleeps whispers Happy nap.

"It's time to lay my egg," clucks flies Meg the hen.

verbs

Read, then answer the questions.

Frank the skunk

Frank is a skunk. If skunks are scared, they run, stop, and stomp their feet. Skunks hiss, squeal, and spray very smelly stuff.

1 What sort of animal is Frank?

  a a skunk   **b** a snake   **c** a spider

2 What is another word for **stomp**?

  a stop   **b** stamp   **c** run

3 Skunks hiss when they are _____ .

  a happy   **b** sleepy   **c** scared

4 Write 4 things skunks do when they are scared.

  1. _____   2. _____

  3. _____   4. _____

5 What would you do if you saw a skunk?

_____

I finished this lesson online.	This egg hatched.	I can recognize action and saying verbs.	I can read

1 Color **ay** words.

| play | cap | tray | say | all |
| kite | way | yay | today | stay |

2 Make **ay** words. Write each word. Read each word.

Milky Way says

ay

d_____   aw_____

p_____   pl_____

sw_____   spr_____

pr_____   tod_____

3 Say the name of each picture. Color its beginning, and ending sound.
Write the word.

  d s h oy ay an _____

  tr cr fr y al ay _____

  sr gr br ay op at _____

  sm fl pl oy ag ay _____

1 Use the wheels to make words. Write the words.

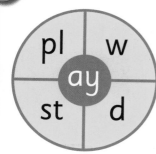

_____

_____

_____

_____

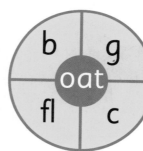

_____

_____

_____

_____

2 Color the **igh** words yellow, **ir** words **red**, **or** words orange, **oad** words green.

(score) (light) (road) (dirt) (girl) (load)

(sight) (sport) (stir) (toad) (wore) (night)

3 Sort the words into their word families.

igh	ir	or	oad

4 Put these words in alphabetical order.

way   day   say   hay

_____   _____   _____   _____

1 Join each word to a picture.

light

day

bird

horse

oats

boat

2 Read the clue. ✎ Write the word.

I have wings. I can fly up high.

I am a b_____ .

I have four legs. I live in a stable.

I am a h_____ .

I help you to see things when it is dark.

I am a l_____ .

I float on water. I carry things and people across the sea. I am a b_____ .

3 ✎ Write a sentence using Milky Way's word.

today _____

_____

_____

ay

1 Match the sentences to the pictures.

Brad walks sideways on his 8 legs.
He scuttles and crawls across the sand.

The lion got a thorn stuck in his paw.
He started to cry.

"I can fly by the light of the sun!"

Brad crashed the truck into a tree.
Bang!

2 Write sentences to match each picture.

_____

_____

_____

_____

_____

_____

I finished this lesson online.	This egg hatched.	I can read and write ay words.	I can read

1 Say the name of each picture. Color the word family.

(or) (ir)   (ay) (igh)   (oa) (ay)   (ight) (ate)

2 Circle the rhyming words in each row.

goat	coat	foot	boat	part	note
soak	seek	joke	park	oak	pick
goal	foal	hill	girl	roll	coal

3 Write the words in the correct order.

wanted   icy   Roary   drink   cold.   an

_____

_____

4 Write the words in the correct box.

water
home
sleep
healthy
growing
food

1 syllable	2 syllables

MAP 12 LESSONS 111 TO 120

Quiz

5 Say the name of each picture. Color its beginning, middle, and ending sound. Write the word.

(ch)(sh)(a)(e)(ll)(lt) _____

(cl)(sl)(o)(i)(ck)(ch) _____

(dr)(gr)(e)(i)(nt)(nk) _____

6 Write:

3 common nouns.

_____   _____   _____

3 proper nouns.

_____   _____   _____

7 Color the saying verbs.

(shouts)   (runs)   (asks)   (hops)   (yells)   (screams)

8 Color the action verbs.

(creeps)   (walks)   (hiss)   (trots)   (sighs)   (pounces)

9 Write a sentence about the picture.

_____

_____

_____

Excellent!

YOU COMPLETED

MAP 12

YOU CAN:

- [ ] Recognize and write **oa** words.
- [ ] Recognize and write words bossy **r** words eg: **ar, er, ir, or,** and **ur.**
- [ ] Read and write **ight** and **ay** word families.
- [ ] Read and write words with blends: **bl, cr, dr, sl, tr, lk, nd, st, mp,** and **ft.**
- [ ] Identify **proper nouns** and **common nouns.**
- [ ] Identify **action verbs** and **saying verbs.**
- [ ] Read these books:

Reading eggs First Grade Workbook

1 Complete the crossword. Use the pictures.

Across

1.
8.
3.
9.
4.
12.
6.

Down

1.
10.
2.
11.
5.
7.

1 Circle the correct word.

tap
tape

dim
dime

kit
kite

can
cane

plane
plan

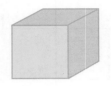

cub
cube

dote
dot

rose
rod

2 Color the picture that matches.

tadpole

eagle

rainbow

drop

beetle

robot

arrow

cook

1 ✏️ Write the missing letters to complete each word.

 _____ark

 _____eese

 _____irt

 _____erry

 b_____

 l___f

 qu_____n

 b___k

 p_____

 fl_____

 fl___t

 b___t

2 Name the picture. ✏️ Write the word.

_____

_____

_____

1 Draw a star ⭐ for each word you know.

me		for		these	
be		so		girl	
green		now		boy	
that		where		say	
there		when		ask	
hello		down		why	
have		up		stay	
they		very		together	
do		who		today	
come		what		Saturday	
my		was		above	
here		with		out	
goes		want		walk	
day		tried		happy	

1 Read the clues. ✏ Write the words.

I have 2 eyes, a nose, and a mouth.
I am a _____ .

I live in the sand.
I have lots of legs.
I am a c_____ .

We eat cheese and say squeak.
We are m_____ .

I have leaves and can grow.
I am a p_____ .

I live in a hole.
My name is Moe.
I am a m_____ .

I am orange. Rabbits like to eat me.
I am a c_____ .

I am a day. I come after Friday.
I am S_____ .

I am a month.
I come after May.
I am J_____ .

I am a small animal.
I carry my shell on my back.
I am a s_____ .

I grow food and look after cows. I don't live in the city.
I am a _____ .

Congratulations

This is to certify

_____

has completed the Reading Eggs First Grade Program.

_____
Date

_____
Signature